Another Hill To Climb

I think it frets the saints in heaven to see how many desolate creatures on the earth have learnt the simple dues of fellowship and social comfort in a hospital.

Elizabeth Barrett Browning

Another Hill
To Climb

Vince Hill

with Nick Charles

First published in the United Kingdom in 2010 by
Bank House Books
PO Box 3
New Romney
TN29 9WJ UK
www.bankhousebooks.com

British Library Cataloguing in Publication Data
A catalogue record for this book is available from the British Library

ISBN 9781904408796

Typesetting and origination by Chandler Book Design

CONTENTS

FOREWORD
by ROLF HARRIS

Vince is what Australians call a good bloke – no side, no tantrums, no unreasonable demands, yet in front of the mike, where it counts, he never fails to deliver the magic that earned him his reputation as 'the singer's singer'.

When you read someone's book of reminiscences, you're always amazed at all the little things, and sometimes huge, earth-shattering things that have affected their lives. In most instances you find you had absolutely no idea of these occurrences, even though they happened at times when you were very close and thought you knew everything about them.

Vince's life has been a huge roller-coaster of a ride, and at times you marvel at the way he has handled it all. You wonder how you would have coped with some of the setbacks. But at the end of the day you've never seen Vince moaning or whingeing. Whatever life threw at him, he just got on with it and did what was needed to get the job done. It's only now that the story *behind* the story can be told.

Nice one, Vince. Good on yer, mate (as they say in the classics).

Rolf

CHAPTER ONE

Remembrance

It is hard to imagine anyone enjoying a stay in hospital either as an out-patient or confined to a bed, but somehow I always thought it profoundly unfair when I heard someone say that they hated the places. All the same, I felt definite insecurity when I realised that the balance of my life was held in a hospital's surgical glove, and I was as helpless as a baby.

This was my second results visit in a year. The first had culminated with the words 'I'm sorry, Mr Hill, but I'm afraid you have tested positive for prostate cancer' – and this time, although there was no particular reason, I felt a feeling of dread that was hard to explain.

I had been greeted by a receptionist in her late fifties, whose approach was very professional until she ruined it by telling me her mother collected all my records. She followed this up with the news that Dr Finella Brito, my consultant, was held up in traffic, and she was very sorry but there could be an hour's delay.

I looked towards my wife Annie for moral support. She said it was best we wait and of course she was right. We sat down on upright but comfortable chairs in the waiting room, and looked around simultaneously for the obligatory magazines. Annie helped herself to one and stuffed *Country Life* into my hands, but my attention had already been caught by a child with plaits and the whitest face I had ever seen. She was accompanied by a woman who I deduced was her mother, although she looked little more than a girl herself; they were the only other people apart from me awaiting their fate. The child was pretty and had a nice smile, which she directed at Annie and me alternately. She was playing with a small doll, which she twisted nervously in her hands. I wanted to say something friendly or paternal, but could think of nothing appropriate as I wondered if she would survive to have a life, marriage and children of her own. In comparison, I thought, I couldn't grumble if my news was bad: I'd had all of those things and a career that had made me rich and famous. We all had to die of something, I'd told myself dozens of times in the previous week.

'Are you all right?' Annie's voice was barely a whisper. I nodded, and wondered why people rarely spoke normally in doctors', dentists' or hospital waiting rooms. I supposed it was out of some sort of respect.

'Are you . . . ?' My voice sounded strangled, and I cleared my throat before adding, 'OK, I mean.' Annie smiled in reply. What a bloody rock she had been, and how lucky I was to have her. One show business friend had told me that his agent had described her as a formidable but scrupulously fair businesswoman, and I remembered the feeling of pride.

'Tessa, please sit down and read your book. Dr Rogerson will be here soon.' The worried mum sitting opposite had inadvertently introduced us to her pale little girl, and I tried a reassuring smile. I wondered what her doctor's excuse would be for being late, and then inexplicably thought of Lilian and Bill, my mum and dad, my sisters Evelyn and Val, my brother Jack and the Prospect pub in Margate. I smiled at the memory of those far-off days, and the wonderful pleasures of our eagerly awaited two week annual holiday in that magical place.

The first time I ever sang in front of an audience was at the Prospect, and the thrill of it would always stay with me. The smell of beer and cigarette smoke was intoxicating, and when everyone stood up to cheer and shout I was well and truly hooked. I wanted that night to last forever.

I came down to earth, of course. I was only fifteen years old, and I had much to learn and the usual rocky roads to negotiate. In the end show business had been good to me and I had no cause to complain, but it wasn't difficult to recall the loneliness of the long-distance singer, despite having the wonderful Annie by my side. My thoughts drifted back through experiences in cabaret and variety in the best and worst venues in the UK, Europe and America, and the times when I had travelled alone, especially in the early days, and I sat with my head against the wall, eyes shut, trying to remember the name of the club where I had first encountered the stark contrast between showtime adulation and the isolation afterwards.

I suppose I was in my early twenties. I'd travelled by train to close the first half of a variety bill: an old trouper on his way down the ladder was topping the bill, while the first act was an up-and-coming pop group, the second a vivacious girl singer. The audience was in a frenzy of excitement. During the interval the compère came to the communal dressing room and told us the old boy had been taken ill, so I was to close the second half in his place: the show had to go on. Much to my delight I went down very well, and a spectacular explosion of electronic starlight brought the evening to a close. Two hours later I was standing alone in the pouring rain on the station platform waiting for my train, which was late as usual, with not another living soul in sight. I shivered as the wind penetrated my stormproof jacket, tossed bits of refuse into the air and made my eyes water. I had other lonely moments, but I will never forget that night on an early morning railway station.

'Tessa Styles? Dr Rogerson will see you now – please come this way. What a lovely dolly you have . . .'

Half of me felt the wind howling along the dank platform, but the other half warmed to the voice of the kindly receptionist, daughter of one of my biggest fans . . . even if she was in her late fifties and her mother in her eighties.

'What a lovely child. I wonder what's wrong with her.' Annie was genuinely moved. I looked at the door that had closed behind mother and daughter and muttered something appropriate, inexplicably reflecting again on the early days of my career, at the wonderful Prospect and at another popular music house, my local pub in Coventry, The Bantam, where I appeared regularly.

I was only six years old when on 14 November 1940 Coventry sustained one of the worst bombing raids of the entire Second World War. Fortunately I, alongside many other young people, had been evacuated, but I have memories of the dreadful scars left on our beloved city and grew up listening to countless tales of the night when a new word entered the English language: Coventration. Home Secretary Herbert Morrison arrived within hours of the all-clear, and two days later King George VI visited the worst-hit areas. The destruction was catastrophic. Archive photographs show piles of rubble where the old city once stood, and well into the late '40s and early '50s the evidence of the carnage was there for all to see. One image stands out for me more than any other: a huge picture of the ruined cathedral. The vivid and hauntingly accurate caption describes the walls that still stood as 'a sentinel towering over the ruined city'.

I remember my mother remarking that some of those who survived the night rarely smiled again, and many felt guilty if they went out to enjoy themselves. 'You could help them forget' she once said, and when I asked how she told me that all I needed to do was sing: 'You have such a wonderful voice.' I didn't take her seriously at the time, but I never forgot her words.

It was hard for me to think of myself as a talented performer. If I was as good as she always told me, why did I have to get up at 5am and go and work down a coal mine? Only one thing was certain: when I was eighteen I would be called up for National Service, which at the very least would rescue me from living like a mole. The reason I had chosen the local colliery in the first place was because working an early morning shift suited my night-time singing commitments around the clubs – but the thought of a lifetime underground horrified me. Even though I worked for the most part in the New Heading Section, essentially haulage, as far as I was concerned I needed rescuing. When I saw an advertisement saying that the Royal Corps of Signals Band wanted a vocalist I decided to apply. My mum wrote the letter, and I got an audition that was a little like *The X-Factor*. I'd barely sung a dozen bars before the musical director asked, 'When do you want to start?' I spent my National Service touring the UK, Europe and even as far afield as Egypt, and when my two years were up they asked me to stay on for a further three months. I had definitely caught the singing for a living bug, and when National Service was over I decided to turn professional.

'Mr Hill, would you like to come through? Dr Brito will see you now.' The receptionist smiled a receptionist's smile and ushered us in. I talked small talk, perhaps in the hope that if she liked me she would make the news better. Dr Brito was shuffling sheets of paper, staring at them over modern spectacles. 'Ah, Mr Hill . . .' she said, looking up, 'please sit down and make yourself comfortable.' We sat down, but I was far from comfortable. I gripped the arms of the chair and waited for the sentence. 'I'm pleased to see that you've got a clean bill of health following the prostate operation twelve months ago.'

I recalled the test results on that occasion, and the terrible words 'prostate cancer' echoing in my ears – exacerbated by the fact that my dear friend Bob Monkhouse had recently succumbed to it. 'We believe we've caught it in time, Mr Hill,' the doctor had said. 'It requires radical surgery and an immediate procedure to remove the prostate gland.' I'd imagined him in his green smock and wellies, wielding an axe rather than a scalpel, and I'd tried to make terror look brave. The reality was routine micro-surgery and I was back on stage a fortnight later. I asked myself for the hundredth time why I felt so bad this time: after all, I felt fine. The only reason I was here at all was because I had accompanied Annie for a blood test and the doctor had decided to include me too.

'As for this latest test, I'm afraid I have to tell you that you've got a condition called chronic myeloid leukaemia, and . . .' The rest of her words were drowned by the orchestra in my brain. I'd obviously done my last show. The fat lady was about to sing.

CHAPTER TWO

The Longest Night

I barely spoke on the way home but I did a lot of thinking, mainly about fellow entertainers I'd known who were now dead. I pondered on the possibilities of an afterlife, and chewed over the names of one or two fixers I'd known who might be celestial agents. Suddenly it became a prospect worth investigating, and I managed a smile at the thought of getting measured for a tuxedo with bits cut out for my wings and perhaps even topping the bill somewhere on high. Then I remembered that Al Jolson, Frank Sinatra and Sammy Davis would probably have a say in that . . .

'Vince, you're going too fast! Slow down!' Annie's voice brought me down to earth, and I complied with her wishes even though I wanted to get home as quickly as possible. My head was full of a variety of thoughts and kept switching from one to another. I had recently read about a billionaire industrialist who had contracted something irreversible and had six months to live; no matter how much money he had, he couldn't buy himself good health. Who was it who said that God had a sense of humour? I couldn't think of too many people I'd harmed, so with any luck that would be taken into account. Then I wondered if I was delirious, or maybe in shock.

Annie came to the rescue. 'Look, we've had trials and tribulations before and come out the other end, and we'll beat this thing together. You heard what the doctor said: there are still more tests, to establish its extent and whether it's treatable. It's not necessarily terminal.

Are you listening, Vince?'

Annie talked sense, so of course I listened. The rest of the day disappeared in a blur of everything and nothing. In the evening we tried to watch a DVD, then had a nightcap, then to bed, then blackness. I lay still in the darkness with my eyes wide open, knowing for sure that sleep was going to elude me and wondering if I should read a book or tackle some of the ever-mounting paperwork in my office. At least the cold, clammy, panicky feeling had receded, and I was no longer contemplating death, athough I continued to think about its inevitability – as we all do from time to time.

I listened to the night sounds and tried to identify the different sounds from the River Thames as it passed under my bedroom window on its way to the sea. Annie and I had bought the house some thirty years before. It had been built next to the mooring of a fabulous houseboat that belonged to the Vanderbilts. When the head of the clan went down with the *Lusitania* in 1915 the land was sold, and the house was named Sagamore after the head of a Native American tribe which had links to the Vanderbilts. According to at least one source Captain John Smith, who explored New England in 1614, maintained that the Massachusetts tribes called their kings 'Sachems' while the Penobscots used the term 'Sagamos', Anglicised as 'Sagamore'. I reflected on the possibility that someone who had perished in the *Lusitania* tragedy had slept in this very room, and wondered what sort of death that must have been.

When U-20 surfaced on the orders of Captain Schwieger less than 10 miles off the coast of Ireland on the afternoon of 7 May, to charge the submarine's batteries, he saw the *Lusitania* in the distance. He had already sunk two other liners, and only had a couple of torpedoes remaining. Schwieger fired just one from a distance of 700 yards, and didn't need the second. The ship went down, and Alfred Vanderbilt and over a thousand others perished in less than twenty minutes.

I listened to the occasional sounds of ducks and geese and the chug of a launch navigating its night passage past my window, the gentle lap of the water against the riverbank just below me resonating a little like percussion. The sounds represented life and living; this would be the last time I would think of dying from leukaemia. Annie was right: we would face it and fight it. I wasn't in the least tired, and returned once more to thinking back over my career.

After eventually leaving the Royal Corps of Signals Band three months after my National Service ended, I took a short tour contract in a musical called *Floradora*. When this ended I heard that the Teddy Foster Band needed a singer, so I applied and was delighted to get the job. Teddy was well known in music circles, up there alongside Joe Loss, Lou Preager, Ambrose, Eric Delaney, Johnny Dankworth, Geraldo, Ted Heath and Jack Hylton. I sang with him for two years and the experience was truly monumental. Subsequently he opted for a female lead singer after discovering Julie Rogers, who later stormed the British charts with 'The Wedding' in 1964. To date it has sold 15 million copies, and counting. Julie and Teddy married, and she worked in such places as Australia, Hong Kong, Singapore, Thailand, Portugal, Holland and Spain, and went on to have three more hits. They remained happily married until poor Teddy succumbed to kidney failure in 1984; she is now happily married to agent Michael Black.

I moved my head sideways, realising that I'd lain on my back in the same position for too long and was as stiff as a board. I rolled onto my side, and thought of Annie and how we had met in Tito Burns's office when I was in my early twenties. Tito was one of London's top agents, responsible for Cliff Richard and the Drifters (later The Shadows), the UK's biggest stars of the time – and he was a thoroughly nice guy. He went on to an executive position at London Weekend Television and was the force behind many major productions. Tito was on my list of 'must be on his books' agents, as he was for all jobbing singers, and when I first met him I discovered I had an additional reason to pay regular visits. Annie Davison, a pretty, shapely and adorable teenager, was his secretary, and it was love at first sight. If I'd had a wish list of all the attributes of my ideal mate she would have ticked every single box, and in a business where divorce and separation are bywords I must have been lucky or blessed. Annie lay peacefully a few inches away, and I had to hold my breath and strain my ears to hear her gentle breathing. We had been together fifty years and I wondered where on earth they had gone to. Looking back, I was lucky to get a second date.

Mine was a generation dominated by Edwardian values and thinking. While it would be wrong, even irresponsible, to paint the epoch as whiter than white, the fact was that many of these values lingered well into the years that were later associated with the emancipation of young people. I was delighted when a smiling Annie accepted my offer of a trip to the pictures, and perhaps relieved if not surprised when she turned up. I was a little apprehensive because I hadn't got much money, and the nearest she was going to get to seeing a film was the cartoon cinema at Piccadilly Circus. Worse was to come: I had to put her on a bus back to her home in East Acton because I hadn't got the taxi fare. We laugh about it to this day, but I'm not sure she's completely forgiven me.

Annie and I married in the famous Caxton Hall in Westminster, venue for so many celebrity marriages, in 1959, and I'm embarrassed to admit that we bent the rules slightly to make this possible. To qualify to be married there you had to live in the area – and of course we didn't. However, Annie's Uncle Arthur was a keeper at Hyde Park, and as part of his job lived at the park's South Lodge. We gave his address. I often joke with Annie that we might not be legally married, having lied on the application, but she's always quick to point out that we lived there for two days, courtesy of Uncle Arthur's insistence on telling the truth.

After leaving Teddy Foster's band I worked the club circuit for a while. One day I bumped into Len Beadle, a musician friend, and over coffee we discussed how we could break into the big-time. Like all performers, our driving force was the desire for stardom, and the cliché on so many of our lips was 'making it'. The idea that Len put to me immediately got my attention. He planned to put together a vocal group, which he'd already decided to call The Raindrops (not to be confused with Ellie Greenwich and Jeff Barry's American outfit, which came later), and there was a place in it for me if I wanted it. He wanted a female lead singer and had chosen Emma Rede, born Jacqueline Norah Flood, from Dublin – where by the age of fourteen she had featured on Radio Eireann. Once she moved to London she was quickly spotted by Ronnie Aldrich, who changed her name to Jackie Lee and made her lead singer with his band The Squadronnaires. After our meeting Len contacted Johnny Worth, who was available after leaving the Oscar Rabin Band, and I made it clear that I wanted in too. Len took up the fourth berth himself, and The Raindrops were born.

We worked hard to put things together, and our efforts paid off. Our first big break came when we were offered a radio slot on the BBC Light Programme (forerunner to Radios 1 and 2): on the very popular programme *Parade of the Pops* we performed our own arrangements of American hits, some of which we recorded with a share of success. As I recall it, we covered Claudine Clark's 'Party Lights' and the Shirelles' 'Will You Still Love Me Tomorrow'. Inevitably, with Jackie Lee fronting the group, we were occasionally credited as Jackie Lee and The Raindrops, and this appeared on the labels of some recordings.

Len Beadle's Raindrops had great potential, and this was eventually born out by our subsequent individual successes. Len was an extremely accomplished musician who later developed into a major force in music publishing. Johnny Worth became a prolific songwriter, who wrote countless hits in the '60s and beyond, and was probably solely responsible for the career success of Adam Faith, having written 'What Do You Want', 'Poor Me', 'How About That' and 'Someone Else's Baby'. Some even say that had there been no Johnny Worth then *Budgie*, one of the most popular TV series of the decade, which brought Faith into everyone's front room as an actor, would never have happened.

Jackie Lee must count as an unheralded pop heroine. In her post-Raindrops career she recorded some splendid stuff, including a song written by Bacharach and David, to say nothing of many popular television commercials. Individual success may have eluded her, but her voice was top of the charts as a backing singer on Tom Jones's 'Green, Green Grass of Home' – and somebody called Elton John was part of her backing group at one stage. Without doubt many will remember her children's TV series favourite hit single

'White Horses', under the name Jackie, and finally, before a vocal condition cut short her career, the children's theme song 'Rupert The Bear', which was a bestseller.

In my head there was a confused, heady, delirious mixture of river water, wildlife sounds, submarines, lifeboats and distant music from a recording studio, which must have been the prelude to eventual sleep. I awoke in daylight from a dream in which I had been in a consulting room with a doctor who was talking words I couldn't understand.

During my next hospital visit it was explained carefully and sympathetically that chronic myeloid leukaemia is a rare form of cancer that affects relatively few people. Myeloid cells start in the spinal cord or the bone marrow, then mature and divide. Unfortunately, as a result of leukaemia, they begin to divide quickly and uncontrollably, which seriously interferes with the immune system and leaves the body wide open to infection. The positive news was that it could be treated with a number of highly specialised drugs, although many patients have to undergo bone marrow or even stem cell transplants. For now I didn't know where my particular version slotted in or what treatment to expect, as I had to undergo more tests, but of one thing I was certain: there would be no feeling sorry for myself; Annie and I would fight this together. The fat lady could get back in her box.

CHAPTER THREE

Doris Duck

Sagamore has a landing stage adjoining the north side of our garden. This leads onto a terrace and is my favourite place. We can roll a canvas canopy over it if there are showers, and the area even retains some heat as the weather cools, which is an unexpected but wonderful bonus. We entertain a lot, and although the house has a marvellous dining room that wouldn't be out of place in the Garrick Club more often than not we elect to eat out on the terrace and watch the river world go by. Sometimes there are tourist boats, and occasionally you hear the guide announcing who lives where. As I sit there with a glass of wine on a summer afternoon, I often wonder if the boatload of foreigners has even the vaguest idea who Vince Hill is.

I stood with my customary bowl of bread for the ducks and watched with fascination as they approached from different directions. As unlikely as it might sound, I recognise many of them, and have dished out daft names along with the bread. Today there was one that I hadn't seen before. Undoubtedly she was the scruffiest duck I had ever seen. It was hard to judge if they were battle scars or if she'd fallen out with her hairdresser, but dragged through a hedge backwards is the phrase that comes to mind. Her head resembled that of an ageing punk, with some bits stuck up and others stuck out, while her feathers looked as if they'd been stuck in by hand – although it was more likely they were on their way out. For a moment I felt a kinship, an alliance between the condemned, but I shook myself out of anything that could lead to self pity and instead made sure that she had the lion's share of my gift. 'Don't worry, Doris,' I said aloud, 'me and you's gonna make it!'

'What's that, Dad?' My son Athol had sneaked up quietly behind me, as he always did on pay days – presumably in case I tried to escape.

'Nothing, son. Just talking to Doris.'

'And you reckon I drink too much,' I heard him say as he wandered off.

Athol was born on a rainy October day in 1971 after Annie had suffered several miscarriages. Our joy was profound, but the pregnancy had not been without trauma.

At three months Annie confided her fears that her stomach swelling wasn't entirely baby, and while it's difficult for any man to imagine how this felt to an expectant mum, the stress and worry for me was immeasurable. We took her fears to her gynaecologist, Victor Lewis, a lovely man who remains a friend to this day, and after tests it was confirmed that she had a tumour, which had to be removed immediately. I spent the entire period in a panic that was worse than any stage fright I'd ever experienced, and the news that the operation had been successful and the tumour wasn't malignant gave me unimaginable relief. The downside was that Annie had to stay in bed for three months, which may not sound like bad news – but the novelty wore off after a couple of days. Dr Lewis offered one concession, however: he allowed her to get up and go out once, but only if he accompanied her. This was so she could attend my opening night at London's Talk of the Town.

Part of my stage show routine was based on a skating scene from the film *Love Story*. In the film skaters danced exquisitely to a beautiful orchestration and when, towards the end of the four week run, I heard the news that Annie had given birth and mum and baby were fine I felt so light-headed it was as though I was dancing on ice myself; I was as proud as it is possible to be. We named him Athol after Athol Carr, a dear friend of ours who owned the Brecon Hotel in Rotherham. The

Brecon was a Mecca for professionals on the cabaret and theatre circuit: Dickie Valentine, Roy Castle, Frankie Vaughan and Matt Munro, to name but a few were all regulars, and Athol Carr did us proud. Many's the time we got back in the early hours to find him propped up in the corner of the bar where he'd nodded off while waiting for us to return. There would follow a nightly ritual of great food, enormous quantities of booze and storytelling that figures in showbiz history. Athol Carr was a legend too, I loved the man and his name and so did Annie, so Athol Hill was our new-born. Another memory about the naming of Athol came to mind as I watched Doris. My lawyer at the time was Roy Friedman, another delightful man, and I recalled his reaction when I told him the name we had decided upon. 'You do realise that some bright Herbert at school is bound to mess with the spelling and determine that an atoll's a hill of sorts? He'll probably be Hill Hill by the time he gets to secondary school.' I pondered on that for a while, and even consulted an encyclopaedia – discovering that Charles Darwin had popularised the term atoll, having described them as 'a subset in a special class of islands, the unique property of which is the presence of an organic reef'. More recently the word had been defined as 'an annular reef enclosing a lagoon in which there are no promontories other than reefs and islets composed of reef detritus'. They started out as underwater volcanic eruptions, which rose above the water as small hills and finally settled down as coral reefs.

I turned away from the river and gazed momentarily as Athol disappeared from view at the end of the driveway; he was such a lovely guy when he was away from alcohol and drugs. When he was on one or both, well that was another story. In all probability, he was the classic example of the offspring trying to find a way in life for himself, while simultaneously following in famous footsteps. He was by no means alone, I knew there were dozens of examples scattered across the globe but the pressures and fallout are much more disturbing when close to home. For the millionth time I pondered on whether we could have done more, or if we had in fact done enough.

I didn't expect him to follow in my exact pattern of musical footsteps by any means, it is accepted that music fashions are forever changing and we are all committed to whatever our personal epoch happens to be; so whether it was a form of rebellion or simply a modern choice I don't know, but Athol was into heavy metal and he chose the drums to hook it onto. He is hugely talented with a great sense of rhythm and his timing is immaculate, there was definitely a time when I thought he might make the breakthrough; but that is his tale to tell.

The other ducks became bored with me giving all the good bits to Doris and decided to swim to currents new, but she seemed content to listen to my ramblings and cocked her head comically. The bowl was empty now. She swam in a circle and, having decided that her lunch and my need for a confidante was at an end, headed for the opposite riverbank some thirty yards distant. I watched with narrowed eyes as she began to slow. After getting nowhere for a minute or two, Doris decided to float downstream with the current. I knew what it was like to tread water, and I hated it.

I walked back to the house, thinking about when The Raindrops dried.

CHAPTER FOUR

When The Raindrops Dried

Three days later a letter arrived from the hospital in the early morning post. I wandered slowly into the kitchen to find a knife to open it.

The kitchen was somewhere I loved. I had taken up cooking some years earlier, and although I have a tendency to favour Thai dishes I experiment constantly with recipes and have developed lots of ideas of my own. I'm a fan of Rick Stein, who's often referred to as a celebrity chef (perhaps a little unfairly given that he ran at least four restaurants), but my inspiration has to be Marguerite Patten. Having advised the government on austerity rationing during the war, honoured 'for services to the art of cookery' by the Queen in 1991, gaining four Lifetime Achievement Awards and being appointed Woman of the Year in 2007, she's a goddess of the kitchen – and a dear friend of ours.

I picked up a knife that had helped prepare a thousand meals and, holding it like a dagger, slit the envelope open and took out a single sheet. It invited me to telephone Hammersmith Hospital to arrange for further blood tests – but it was the word 'oncology' that made the greatest impression. I knew from my prostate experience that this meant the cancer department, and I suspect it strikes a certain sense of dread into all those summoned to attend. I folded the letter carefully and placed it next to the phone.

Crossing the breakfast room, I switched on the news. A journalist was standing outside the House of Commons in the pouring rain reporting on some political issue or another, and I noticed that a few rogue raindrops had sneaked onto the camera lens. My thoughts returned to our singing group, and I was startled to realise that something so vital and important to me and my career had paled into insignificance in light of recent events. I felt a little ashamed, and concentrated harder on my recollections.

'You and I are the engine room in this outfit, Vince.' Johnny Worth's voice was so real in my head that I looked up, half-expecting to see him standing there. We'd been having private words about Raindrops politics, and I'd confided that Annie with her agency hat on was trying to get me to leave and go solo. For Johnny's part he was fed up with the bickering between Jackie Lee and her then husband Len Beadle, over her rumoured affair with a young man in Bernard Delfont's office. I was more concerned over the fact that she wanted her beau to leave Delfont and take over as The Raindrops' road manager: that meant less money for all of us, and there wasn't much of it as it was.

'For God's sake, Vince, see sense!' In my imaginings Annie's voice rang out as loudly as Johnny's. She had been waving her 'go solo' flag for months, but basically I was very nervous of the prospect. The reality was that The Raindrops had projected me (and the others) to another level, and important people in the business were beginning to notice us. The prospects for me as a solo artist were good, but did I have the bottle? For someone like me, who admits loving the smell of the grease paint and the roar of the crowd, it's difficult to explain to others how one can fear doing the very thing you love most of all. But I suffered considerably from pre-show nerves, not that anyone would have guessed – I always seemed as calm as a cucumber.

Professional entertainers are infamously insecure, and I was no exception. In a way the group thing, while not solving my stage fright, gave me a kind of protective shield, even though there was actually more at stake. Not only did you make yourself look bad if you loused something up, you let down the team. I'd always had to draw on massive reserves of courage before a performance, but I was fine as soon as I was out there in front of the crowd, and the high from performing was my drug of choice. But could I overcome my apprehension and muster up the courage to go to another level on my own?

The Raindrops were very well known in those halcyon days, during which the building blocks for today's popular music industry were put in place, and a solo career would be at the same level. Now, when the radio dial's littered with music programmes and homes have access to nigh on a thousand TV stations, it's impossible to imagine the attention you gained in the late '50s or early '60s by appearing on the only major radio station or on one of only two TV stations, BBC or ITV. Inevitably this could work both ways, and the British public could make or break artists. A good example of the latter concerns Terry Dene and Edna Savage, who were briefly Britain's number one celebrity couple. Dene's National Service was deferred because of contractual commitments, and when he joined up it was handled so badly by the press that his career was almost ruined: from thousands of adoring fans mobbing the couple everywhere they went they disappeared into obscurity virtually overnight.

The '50s were a time of post-war austerity, with wartime meat rationing, for example, lingering on until midnight on 4 July 1954. It was a dull and miserable period for many, and by the middle of the decade the younger generation were dying to break out. Rock 'n' Roll was beginning to develop in America, but this was initially suppressed to some extent by the powers that be in the UK, and for a while we had to content ourselves with skiffle – in which Lonnie Donegan reigned supreme, selling 3 million copies of 'Rock Island Line' in 1956.

By 1957 times had changed to such a degree that Prime Minister Harold Macmillan said in a speech to fellow Conservatives, 'Let us be frank about it: most of our people have never had it so good.' In 1959 the television-owning public numbered in excess of 25 million, exceeded only by the Americans, even though we only had the choice of two channels. This meant that popular entertainers regularly entered the homes of the vast majority of the population. In shops, factories and other places of employment, sound and conversation were based on popular music more often than not, and while a young thing called Elvis and an outrageous dynamo known as Little Richard had earlier reinvented popular music, great exponents of ballads and fun songs were still there well into the '60s and beyond. To draw an analogy, a single popular music personality could dominate in the screens in the late '50s and early '60s in the way that only something like the death of Lady Diana or a disaster on the scale of 9/11 does today. So The Raindrops, on the radio every day and featuring regularly on television, were as popular as other top performers of the era.

In the event, parting company with the group was fairly simple and relatively pain free, I turned up at a rehearsal and informed them I'd received an offer I couldn't refuse. This was the truth, thanks to Annie's hard work in the background, and it was an amicable parting. In the summer of 1961 I did my last show with The Raindrops on my home ground at the Coventry Theatre, with Shirley Bassey, Ken Dodd and the Three Monarchs.

Now I had to face my stage fright demons at another level, and with hindsight I was as ready as it was possible to be. My first solo show in the upper stratosphere of professional cabaret was at the Astor Club in Berkeley Square, which was highly fashionable at the time. Amid my recollections, I clearly remember setting out to tackle it with all the confidence and professionalism I could muster, given that I'd only heard about it at the eleventh hour.

I walked across the kitchen and shuddered slightly, either because I was recalling my first top line solo show, or because I'd returned to the telephone and my recently opened letter. I was unsure. I put my hand on it and leaned forward into the sunlight from the kitchen window, and thought of Mike Yarwood, famous for his legendary impressions of Harold Wilson – and also for his battle with stage fright. We'd worked together a few times, and although we were never close friends I liked him, while Annie had got on particularly well with his wife Sandy. I thanked my lucky stars that my problem with audiences had been nothing like his. One gig sticks out particularly in my memory. We'd been booked by Billy Marsh at London Management to do a show at the eminent Uppingham College, and an hour before we were due on stage the organisers received a message that Mike wasn't going to make it. Word trickled through that it wasn't the first time this had happened, and the reason was extreme stage fright. The story goes that poor Mike thought he'd gone some way to solving his problem by having a few drinks, but a few became a few too many, resulting in alcoholism and the end of both his marriage and his career. 'There but for the grace of God . . .' I muttered under my breath, at the same time dialling the number on the hospital letter.

The phone was answered by a beautiful female voice. I suppose I was expecting the usual pleasant but pragmatic receptionist type, but this one was chatty, with a slight trace of a chuckle. Perhaps I'd just interrupted the tag line to a joke she'd been telling, or she was blessed with a trace of Alma Cogan (known as 'The Girl with the Giggle in her Voice'), but whatever the reason I found myself suitably cheered. 'You're the singer, aren't you?' she said happily. How much nicer this was than 'You used to be Vince Hill, didn't you?', 'My mother thought you were dead' or, most recently, 'I saw one of your records in a charity shop!' We exchanged pleasantries, and I carefully noted my appointment date in my diary.

As I replaced the receiver I thought of Alma Cogan. Maureen Lipman is reported to have described her as 'the first English Jewish star', and I haven't a clue how to describe the extent of her fame to a modern generation. This extraordinary singing phenomenon was born in Golders Green and brought up on jazz music. She originally sang with the Ted Heath Band at tea dances before she was in her teens, but her big break came when Vera Lynn recommended her to the Grand Theatre in Brighton. One of the most influential DJs of the era was Jack Jackson, and it was he who helped Alma into radio.

To put her achievements into context, I must quote writer Denis Norden: 'In those days, stars were made from radio, and there are no television stars today who are as big as radio stars were then.' Alma starred in *Gently Bentley* and *Take It From Here*, written by Norden, but he has since said that she was so good that she would have 'burst forth anyway'.

Alma's recording career exploded in 1954 with the single 'Bell Bottom Blues', which sold 100,000 copies, and she went on to have eighteen hits in the UK alone, more than any other female artist in the '50s. She was the first ever British female singer to have her own TV series, and the public interest created by her flamboyant dress sense, with masses of material, sequins, narrow waists and beautiful colours, was what legend is made of. More, Alma sang with a laugh in her voice that was so distinctive that you only had to listen to a few words of any song to know it was her. My friendly receptionist would probably never know, but she had a great gift: she only had to speak to put a chuckle into someone's heart.

I turned the TV off and looked out through the window at the sunshine. It was slightly watery, but so far we were escaping the deluge I'd seen on the news. The Thames was strangely deserted. Fleetingly I wondered where the other Raindrops were. Len had passed on to the choir in the sky, but dear Johnny was still around, and the last I had heard of Jackie was that she had gone to live in Canada.

It was just before I left The Raindrops that I met Alma. We were attending a charity bash at a hotel in Bournemouth, and we chatted over a glass of wine and canapés. Annie had mentioned I was leaving the line-up to go it alone, and Alma, who confided to Annie that she was psychic, whispered, 'I know he's leaving them, and I also know he's going to be a star ... and I'll be at his first show.' She went on to explain that at birth her head had been covered by a caul, an afterbirth membrane, and as a result her family had accepted she was blessed with a spiritual gift. At no time did either of us mention the Astor Club, and as far as I'm aware it was never billed as my first solo show. I didn't even know myself until the beginning of the week in question, because Annie and my agent Michael Black hatched a plan to beat my stage fright. I'd worked the Astor Club on several occasions with The Raindrops, and Michael was forever ringing me up asking me to do it solo. At the time I was working hard on my cabaret act and truly believed it was far from ready, so I used this as an excuse; but Annie and Michael were having none of it. I'll never forget Annie pushing the London evening paper entertainment page under my nose one Monday morning. 'There . . . what do you think?' And I read, 'The Astor Club proudly presents for the coming week . . . Vince Hill.' They both knew it was nerves holding me back, and in truth I was as ready as I was ever likely to be. It was lucky they did, otherwise I'd probably still be rehearsing.

When I came off stage to rapturous applause, with tears in my eyes, the first person to congratulate me was Alma Cogan, accompanied by Lionel Bart of Oliver fame. 'I told you so,' she said, 'and I wouldn't have missed it for the world.'

I chuckled at the absurdity of it all, and decided I needed some stimulating conversation . . . so I went out to feed Doris Duck.

CHAPTER FIVE

Bid For Fame

I chose two of the worst winters on record to make my bid for fame. 1961–2 was bad enough, but the winter of 1962–3 was the coldest in England and Wales since 1740. Depressions reached the south of the British Isles, and their fronts brought snow to England, Wales and the southernmost parts of Scotland. As I remember it, the worst winter began abruptly just before Christmas 1962. The records show that the first three weeks of December were changeable and sometimes stormy, and from the 4th to the 6th London experienced its worst spell of fog since the Great Smog of 1952. By 30 December there were snowdrifts 18ft deep and villages were cut off, some for days. Roads and railways were blocked, telephone wires were brought down, stocks of food ran low, farmers couldn't reach their livestock and thousands of sheep, ponies and cattle starved to death. Just about everyone who was there will have a story to tell. One musician friend of mine was travelling down to London from the Midlands on the M1, and remembers bouncing from one 20ft snowdrift wall to another. It seemed that everything was paralysed, and the country ground to a halt. Oh, happy days.

When Annie and I were first married we rented a house from the Salvation Army at Sevenoaks in Kent. The previous tenant had been Johnny Worth. We knew Johnny was leaving it to return to his family's home, and so we seized the moment to apply for the tenancy. By the time the 1962–3 winter set in we had moved on, and were installed in our own home in Worcester Park, Surrey. It was a small detached house that I'd describe as having two and a half bedrooms, but we were proud of our first acquisition. As you'll imagine, it was with considerable dismay that by the first week in January we found ourselves totally frozen up, with no water whatsoever and power cuts to boot. No-one got away unaffected in that winter, I'm absolutely sure. Despite all this I've got no recollection of empty venues – in fact quite the opposite. I can only assume that rather than freeze at home people somehow found their way to a show and kept warm together.

I wouldn't describe the attitude of the remaining Raindrops to me as acrimonious, but there was certainly an undercurrent. What happened next did nothing to improve things. The group was very well established as a result of our success on *Parade of the Pops*, and when he heard I was leaving, its producer Johnny Kingdon took me to one side. 'You do realise that you'll lose your spot on the show if you leave the group, don't you?' I told him I did and that I regretted the loss, but it was something I had to do and the decision was made. I liked Johnny, but explained that my mind was truly made up.

My replacement was John Padley, late of the Jones Boys, who at the time was married to actress/dancer Anne Hart, now Mrs Ronnie Corbett. I was still in the studio when they did their first run-through. I could feel an atmosphere developing, but couldn't quite put my finger on why. Then I saw Johnny Kingdon in a huddle with his assistant producer Pam Cox, and a couple of the little Girl Fridays started running around frenetically. I decided it was time for me to go, and edged towards the door. I got as far as reception when one of them rushed up to me breathlessly and asked if I'd go back, as Mr Kingdon wanted to speak to me. I couldn't have guessed why in a million years.

It transpired that Johnny didn't like The Raindrops' new sound, and gave them an ultimatum: either they took me back into the line-up for the *Parade of the Pops* recordings or they were out of the show. On their behalf Len Beadle declined, saying they'd go their own way. Then, shock of shocks, Johnny offered me a contract to front the programme with the intention of building the show around me. I couldn't believe my luck, but I felt sorry for the others: it had never been my intention to impede their progress.

There followed a whirlwind of professional engagements the like of which I could never have imagined. *Parade of the Pops* had always been high on the list of young people's favourite popular music shows, but Johnny now introduced wholesale changes that made it the nation's number one music show for a while. Every fan of pop music listened to it. If this wasn't enough, I appeared regularly on radio's famous *Saturday Club* and also *Easy Beat*, and covered thousands of miles on sleeper trains to appear in cabaret all over the country. The phone never stopped ringing.

Doris and her mates quickly devoured their daily bread and I made my way back to the kitchen, pausing from my meanderings to pick up my diary. I suddenly realised that my oncology appointment was the day after tomorrow, Wednesday the 7th. It was still just before 8am, so I decided to take the letter up to Annie with her tea and toast, at the same time reflecting on the run up to my first recording contract.

It all began when I managed to land a lucrative sideline, recording demonstration discs for Bob Kingston at Southern Music (now Peer Music), one of the largest music publishing companies in the world. They presented songs to the singers they were trying to attract with quickly produced renditions on acetate discs (not the regular cellulose 45rpm records), recorded by singers who could learn songs quickly and usually put them down in a single take. I could do just that: 'You hum it and he'll sing it straight back' was how they described me. I must have done hundreds at £5 to £10 a go, good money for old rope in the early '60s. My fame in this department soon spread, and in no time at all I was providing the same service for several independent producers, such as Leslie Bricusse, and other companies too. In addition, over a three year period I did so many TV commercial jingles that it seemed my voice was on the telly every time I switched it on. My mentor in the jingle business was Cliff Adams, who most will remember from the Cliff Adams Singers; he remained a close friend until his death in October 2001. As a result of his influence my voice became the sound of Wonder Loaf, 'Drinka Pinta Milka Day', 'Keep Going Well, Keep Going Shell' and Kellogg's Cornflakes, to name but a few. When I look back over the meticulous diary kept by Annie, I wonder how I managed to do it all. The reality was sheer hard work, and at one stage I went a whole decade without taking a holiday. I was to pay a high and terrifying price for this.

One day Bob Kingston called me into his office at Southern Music and asked if I was still on good terms with my ex-Raindrop colleague Johnny Worth, who was now a prolific writer of chart material. I was: Johnny and I were the best of friends and spoke regularly. 'Get him to write you a song, and we'll pay for the session and see to the distribution deal.' I needed no further bidding, and spoke to Johnny that very night. I don't think the significance of his success as a songwriter had properly registered with me: he was just a mate. With hindsight, it was probably naïve of me not to have thought of approaching him myself. After all, he was writing hits at the rate of one a week. How on earth could a singer with my aspirations of fame be buddies with the Paul McCartney of the day and yet not think of begging for a song? The only excuse I can offer is that I was so busy with my own work that I hadn't had time to consider it. Less than a week after my phone call to him, the manuscript for 'The River's Run Dry' landed on my doormat in a brown manila envelope.

Bob Kingston was pleased with the song, and when I saw the arrangement that had been put together by orchestrator Johnny Keating, a close friend of Johnny's, I was convinced I had a major hit on my hands. Keating's shimmering effect from the string section made the hairs stand up on the back of my neck, and produced an awesome background to a great production.

During the relatively short time I'd been working professionally from my London base, Lady Luck had seemed to be permanently on my side. Not only had I married the girl of my dreams, but something seemed to come out of every audition and virtually everything I applied for. Under my breath I continually muttered 'Can it really be as easy as this?' But on one occasion during my early days I was almost led into a nightmare contractual situation. I'd turned up for an open audition at the Astor Club, long before I appeared there professionally. The Arthur Lowe Agency, not to be confused by him of *Dad's Army* fame, was run from there by Michael Black for Bertie Green. Black was in charge when I arrived, and as soon as he'd heard a dozen or so bars he called a halt and shouted for Bertie to come and have a listen. Green liked what he heard and he was all over me like a rash, shoving a piece of paper under my nose together with a pen. 'Sign for me, my boy. I'll get you a recording contract and make you a star.' The more I looked at the document I'd signed the more panicky I felt: I knew I'd done the wrong thing. As I walked slowly towards Piccadilly my emotions switched from euphoria to doom.

As I approached the Circus I suddenly remembered a conversation I'd had with Ian Bevan years before at impresario Harold Fielding's office, shortly after I'd left the army. After my audition with him Fielding had said that he didn't feel he had any suitable work for me at that time, but I was probably the best singer he'd ever heard that he wouldn't be able to use. Before I left, the kindly Ian Bevan (his right-hand man) told me that if I ever needed any advice of any sort not to hesitate to call. Today I definitely needed advice.

With more of a sense of urgency I made my way to Fielding's plush offices in the Haymarket , hoping that Ian Bevan would be there and prepared to see me. I was in luck. He sat me down and read the contract carefully. Finally he placed it on the desk, and said it was the worst possible legal arrangement I could have entered into. Bevan explained it was completely one sided: Bertie Green wasn't responsible for providing anything, but I had to pay him his percentage no matter how I came by the work or where I earned my money from. I was angry and gutted. There was a brief silence before Bevan told me to go back to the Astor Club. 'Work yourself up into as angry a state as you possibly can, and tell him what you think of him and his contract. Tell him it's a one way ticket in his direction, you don't want him or his f***** management, and you want it cancelled immediately'. He added that he knew Green well – and felt that with a little luck he'd react angrily and cancel the agreement.

By the time I arrived back at the Astor I'd worked myself up into a frenzy and did as advised, smashing the document down on Green's desk and telling him to sign underneath where I had written 'cancelled'. With a flurry of foul language he signed, at the same time telling me never to darken his door ever again. I left in triumph and with not a little relief.

Some months later a young singer called Matt Munro was not so lucky. He had signed on the dotted line and years later, whilst sitting on the top of the UK charts, paid Bertie Green many thousands of pounds to buy back his contract.

There would be no such problem with 'The River's Run Dry'. The record deal was an independent contract drawn up with everyone's best interests considered, and I couldn't have been more pleased by Johnny Keating's arrangement. Even so, I was amazed when in no time at all I received a phone call from Pye Records to tell me that I'd entered the top 50 with my first ever recording. Could it really be this easy . . . ? I didn't think so, somehow, and this feeling was borne out when it disappeared from sight the next week. It re-emerged the following week two places higher, before finally disappearing altogether. Nonetheless it was a bright start, and doors began to open as a result. My bid for fame was well underway.

CHAPTER SIX

Starring At
Hammersmith Hospital

We arose early, breakfasted in virtual silence and drove with minimal conversation towards London to keep my appointment at the Hammersmith Hospital. Annie asked from time to time if I was OK, but I was deep in thought.

We already knew that our dear friend Bob Monkhouse had prostate cancer. Such announcements always gained media attention, and his tragic news, which we now heard officially on the car radio, provoked in me thoughts of the unknown thousands everywhere who were enduring potentially life-threatening conditions. Some would be suffering alone. News of their impending death would not be broadcast, and they would not be prayed for by millions. I hoped, nevertheless, that announcing the plight of the famous to the world would inspire prayers for sick people everywhere. I was beginning to see life and death differently, and was never more conscious of the fragility of our human form, which so many of us take for granted, as I was at that moment.

I hate people who wallow in self pity, and never cease to be amazed that those who'd be perfectly entitled to feel a little victimised by destiny are more often than not those who respond positively to personal tragedy. The courageous mother, dying of cancer, who raised tens of thousands of pounds cycling impossible distances to raise money to help others springs immediately to mind. Then there's the terrifyingly young and incredibly brave little girl who refused potentially life-saving treatment so that she could enjoy time at home with her family rather than the pain of continual tests and chemotherapy, which she had experienced for the whole of her short life. My first reaction when I read about her was that I must do something to help, but rationally I soon realised that she didn't actually want anything other than to be normal for a month or two.

The traffic was heavy, and it took almost an hour and a half for a relatively short trip. We parked easily, and found the waiting room. It was heaving, a stark contrast to the one I'd been in a few days before, and I thought again of the countless thousands who had dominated my thoughts in the car.

After what seemed an endless wait, but was probably no more than an hour or so, my name was called and we were taken into a large consulting room. I was greeted by Professor Jane Apperley, who immediately put me at ease. She explained about chronic myeloid leukaemia, the various tests she intended to do, and how they would help her decide the best treatment for me. I listened intently, asking questions from time to time, and began to feel mentally stronger and more optimistic by the minute. The professor, who I would soon be addressing as Jane, ended with a flourish: 'We may have to include an autograft,' she said, standing up.

'Oh!' I said, startled by this turn of events. 'Do you have a pen and a piece of paper? . . . Err . . . what would you like me to write?'

She stared at me for a moment, perplexed, then looked down at my notes. 'Oh! I see,' she said, 'you're a singer . . .' She quickly recovered. 'An autograft is a tissue transplant from one part of your body to another. It's sometimes called an auto transplant. Perhaps we should use that term from now on . . .'

At the time I didn't know whether to laugh or cry, but I've eaten out on the story a few times since, and I'm still not sure if I was put down or not!

I was a captive audience for almost three hours. Much was explained and blood tests were done. One procedure was a little scary, to say the least. I was made to lie down with a tube connected to a vein in my arm, and watched intently as the blood was transported through a machine, then passed back into my body through the other arm. A friendly nurse explained that my white cells concentration was very high, and the machine performed a sieving process. The charming Professor Apperley returned and sat down to enjoy a game of pass the blood with me, while explaining the complexities of my condition. She told me about a tablet called Glivec which I had to take once a day, after lunch or at least after food.

'Philadelphia chromosome or Philadelphia translocation, so named as a result of the location of its research origin, is a specific chromosomal abnormality that is associated with chronic myeloid leukaemia . . .' She knew her stuff and never failed to explain the medical jargon. Unforgivable, I know, but for me it was too much information. I wanted to be treated and I wanted to become well again. Unlike many people I didn't want the sordid details. If I was going to die prematurely I had absolutely no desire to be educated into the whys and wherefores. Annie and I had discussed it, and I knew she would protect me as much as she could.

'It's the result of a reciprocal translocation between chromosome 9 and 22 . . .' I heard Jane's voice but not the words – and the music played . . .

The Johnny Keating Orchestra's violins shimmered in my head. There was a slight echo, characteristic of the time, which beautifully complemented an unforgettable production that is undiminished even today.

The Jaguar's engine was hardly audible and the suspension swallowed the road surface as I swallowed Jane's pills, yet Annie had to repeat her question three times before it registered. I was exhausted: the mental strain was so debilitating that I guessed this alone was responsible for the way I felt. 'Yes, we've got every reason to be optimistic,' I replied. 'Do you think you should give Jackie a ring now they've gone public about Bob's cancer?'

Jackie and Annie went back to schooldays. The girls' respective mums worked together at the local laundry in East Acton in order to pay for their girls' education, Jackie at Burlington Grammar School at the top of Du Cane Road and Annie at the private Godolphin

& Latymer School. I could tell from Annie's sombre manner that it wasn't just our visit to the hospital that was bothering her; she was hurting for her pal, whose husband's diagnosis was infinitely worse than anything that had happened to us.

'I will, but I don't want to say too much about your health, Vince.' She spoke so quietly that I could barely hear her. 'You've already had the all-clear, and prostate cancer's going to kill poor Bob. I don't think I'll mention your recovery. It would be inappropriate, don't you think?'

I nodded, but was busy re-running Jane Apperley's words in my mind. 'Although I'll have to wait for your test results, I have to say that I'm fairly optimistic after what I've seen so far.'

Three months later Bob was dead. Not only did Jackie lose the love of her life, but the industry lost a comedy genius.

Inexplicably I started to hum a tune called 'One More for the Road', written for the musical *The Sky's The Limit* by Johnny Mercer and Harold Arlen. I quickly realised I'd sung it the last time I'd worked with Bob, and it was one of his favourite songs. Like me, Bob loved great traditional production numbers, and both Mercer and Arlen excelled in this department. Sinatra's version of the song is legendary. If you think of 'That Old Black Magic' and 'Summer Wind' for Mercer, and 'Somewhere Over The Rainbow' and the rest of the songs from *The Wizard of Oz* for Arlen, there's no reason to say more.

'*Stars and Garters*,' I suddenly said.

'Pardon?'

'One of Bob's favourite songs was "One More for the Road" and I sang it on *Stars and Garters*. Do you remember?'

'No,' Annie said dismissively, 'but I do remember what a beautiful girl your co-star Kathy Kirby was.' I did too, and how such a talent could have retired so early in her career still remains a mystery to me.

I tried to recall how I'd become involved with *Stars and Garters*, and remembered Daphne Shadwell. Her father, Charles, was conductor of the BBC Variety Orchestra and she and her husband John Hamilton were co-directors of a new variety show project which was intended to emulate the typical pub/club entertainment of the day. The idea of a variety show in such a setting wasn't new: *Café Continental* ran from 1947 till 1953. This was the brainchild of Henry Caldwell, based on a theme he had first used in the Middle East with ENSA (Entertainment National Service Association). One of his biggest coups was to attract Josephine Baker, the famous star of the Folies Bergères. Another possible inspiration for *Stars and Garters* was a 1962 documentary called *Time, Gentlemen, Please*, in which Daniel Farson examined public house entertainment in London. *Stars and Garters* was presented in 1963 by Associated Rediffusion, and was voted best TV series for that year.

When I look back I realise it wasn't one single thing that opened the doors of fame. The Raindrops and *Parade of the Pops* were huge, of course, and all my other radio work culminating with 'River's Run Dry' played a major role, but *Stars and Garters* was perhaps most influential in establishing me as a regular face on television.

As *Stars and Garters* came to the end of its run Johnny Worth rang me. He had written a song called 'Day At The Seaside' for Lonnie Donegan, still a huge star, but he was dragging his feet and Johnny was on a deadline. The song was for a gala night at which our entry for the Eurovision Song Contest was chosen: six singers performed their songs to the nation and the viewers sent in their votes by post. Lonnie couldn't decide whether to be in or not and I was next on the list. I wasn't in the least offended at being second choice, as Johnny and I were mates and there was a kind of we're all in it together mood back then. In any event the song was unsuccessful on the night, but the TV exposure was fantastic and undoubtedly did my bid for fame a power of good.

'It was a shame that *Stars and Garters* ended the way it did.' I replied with a nod. Variety underwent something of a renaissance in the early 1960s as a result of the popularity of pub entertainment. There was a certain magic about the smoky atmospheres, the clinking of glasses, alcohol-induced laughter and the general hubbub that produced an infectious ambience. Couple this with good quality entertainment and it was an irresistible combination. But could it work on television again? A pilot show was suggested, and sadly this was less than successful; in fact co-director John Hamilton described it as a disaster. The troubles began with the attempt to recreate a local pub atmosphere in the studio. The audience of extras, promised a televised night of entertainment at the pub, expected free booze, but were presented with weak cordial and coloured water. The disapproval of the pub 'regulars' was so obvious to the live television viewers that it distracted from the entertainment, and eventually turned the proceedings into chaos. After this, a decision was taken to employ professional extras instead, which went some way towards solving the problem – although regulars were also brought in from a real pub, the Rising Sun, which also contributed the Don Harvey Trio, backing genuine pub singers. Ray Martine was hired as the compère and the Alan Braden Band backed big-name guests. Rediffusion paid Dick Vosburgh, Marty Feldman and Barry Cryer, among others, to clean up Ray Martine's act. Martine, a quick-witted East End comic who appeared regularly at the Deuragon Arms in Hackney, had an act that was so blue it was totally unsuitable for television – but he had a perfect earthiness for the role.

As the charming but unsophisticated *Stars and Garters* took a hold on the TV ratings, I read regularly in the press that it had turned Kathy Kirby and Vince Hill into television stars, and although I didn't feel like one financially or otherwise life was never quite the same for either of us. Soon afterwards Kathy was riding high in the charts with 'Secret Love', and while 'River's Run Dry' didn't live up to its early promise, it was widely played on the radio; this and subsequent recordings provided a certain impetus for my television appearances. Johnny Worth's 'Day At The Seaside', while not a big seller, was forever being played, and someone once remarked that there was no need to buy it because all you had to do was turn on the radio. Success in the entertainment industry is all about putting yourself about, and my songs at this time were pivotal. I followed up 'The River's Run Dry' on the Piccadilly label with 'There You Go', 'Day At The Seaside', 'As It Was Written',

'Blue Velvet', 'If You Knew' and 'It's Only Make Believe'. Then in 1965 I signed for Columbia Records.

I came off the motorway and drove through Henley-on-Thames, carefully keeping to the 30mph speed limit. Today's news was not conclusive, but as I drew into the drive the sun came from behind a cloud.

'Shall we eat out or are you going to conjure something up?'

I turned the question over for a moment or two, then made a decision. 'Let's eat out. I really don't feel like having to cook right now. We've got a lot to talk about – and anyway . . . I have to feed Doris!'

CHAPTER SEVEN

Dipsy Duck

Doris and her cronies were nowhere to be seen when I arrived with my bowl of goodies. I had popped into a local pet shop the day before and purchased a seed feed that the proprietor insisted was perfect for ducks. Now I looked at it critically, wondering if she'd got wind of her dietary change and had gone somewhere else for dinner.

I scanned the Thames in both directions, leaning forward to check the inlets, but there wasn't a duck or swan in sight. I was considering the possibility that there might be a river bird convention happening somewhere when a loud, wailing lament came from the orchard. I had to investigate!

For many years I thought that the orchard had been around for ever. Then one day a man named Barry Spratt appeared at the door. He told me his family had lived at Sagamore during the first year or so of the Second World War. He was an affable and delightful man, and I invited him in. When we offered him a glass of wine from the cellar he said, 'My God! We used to hide down there during the air raids.' I'd not been aware of air raids affecting Lower Shiplake and said so, and he was quick to point out that the Luftwaffe followed the Thames in order to get to vital industrial targets. 'My brother and I used to count them as they flew over,' Barry explained. He said they'd recorded each one by making a pencil mark on the cellar's white-painted brickwork.

When Annie and I first viewed Sagamore we took particular interest in the wine cellar: we both had an interest in good wines and wished to pursue our hobby. The first thing I noticed were these marks on the walls, and I asked the owner what they were. It had transpired that they'd been there when he'd bought the property, and for reasons he was unable to explain he couldn't bring himself to paint over them. Annie and I had now lived in Sagamore for thirty years, and we couldn't bring ourselves to erase them either. Now Barry Spratt had solved the mystery.

I was fascinated by the story, finding myself transported back to my childhood home in Coventry – and the devastation that the Luftwaffe had unleashed upon it. I suddenly realised as I walked towards the din in my orchard that Coventry was almost directly north of Sagamore, so our lovely home had probably featured in the landmarks that led the Luftwaffe to all but destroy my place of birth. It was disturbing.

The charming Barry Spratt told us that his brother, who had shared so many fearful wartime nights with him, went on to become Sir Greville Spratt, Lord Mayor of London. The pleasure on Barry's face when he saw their childhood markings on the wine cellar walls was a joy to behold.

As I approached the orchard the incomprehensible noises were getting louder. As I rounded a clump of bushes the strangest sight came into view, and I stood stock still in an attempt to take it all in. A raggle-taggle rabble of a dozen or so ducks surrounded Doris, who was in even more disarray than usual. I stood there, surveying the spectacle, for a while, wondering how they had got into such an extraordinary state. One muddy creature was lying on its back, legs in the air and looking for all the world as if it was ready for the pot. Another was walking backwards, struggling to stay on its feet. A third seemed to be boss-eyed. The noise stopped as soon as they saw me, and those who were capable eyed me suspiciously. They were in a kind of unequal semi-circle, surrounded by dozens of rotting windfalls beneath two apple trees. There was an odd, pungent, piquant scent in the air that was not entirely objectionable, and was also vaguely familiar. Suddenly the penny dropped . . . the windfalls were fermenting: the smell was alcohol. Doris and her mates were drunk!

'You bloody birds! If you try swimming in that state, you'll drown . . . the whole bloody lot of you!'

'Hi, Vince . . . everything all right?' Jack Crossley, my next-door neighbour, had obviously heard me talking to Doris and the rest of the rabble, and was peering through a gap in the hedge.

'Oh, hi,' I said, trying to look and sound as normal as I could while surrounded by a dozen drunken ducks. 'I bought some new feed from the pet shop, but they don't seem to be hungry.'

Jack looked through the hedge at the horde surrounding me, and then at the apples. 'Probably 'cos they're pissed,' he said, and went on his way.

I threw the seed on the ground in disgust and walked back to the house, wondering if Barry Spratt was still alive and well. I had always assumed that the orchard had been there for generations, but Barry explained that when he lived in the house the garden had been two-tiered, with a lawn on one level and a tennis court on the other. I recalled that a few metal and wooden struts and odd bits of rotting nets had still been in evidence when we moved in all those years ago, and I'd never realised what they were. Sagamore had history, mystery, and undoubtedly many stories to tell.

CHAPTER EIGHT

The Sound of Music

A couple of days later Annie shouted up to me that it was a lovely day, so why didn't I join her on the terrace. I was oblivious of the fine weather. I'd lost track of time and was absorbed in the attic, looking through boxes and boxes of press cuttings, memorabilia and showbiz correspondence dating back to the early '60s. Annie and I were seriously thinking of downsizing, not because we didn't love Sagamore but because we were two people rattling around in a ten-bedroom, eight-bathroom mansion, with servants' quarters and enough Thameside mooring to hold our own regatta. I suppose I was making a token start by deciding what could be dumped and what should be kept. I had to do it while I was in the mood.

Like any large property, Sagamore demands attention. We did nothing like as much entertaining as we'd done in the past, so huge parts of the house remained unused. It seemed a sin. The house deserves to be lived in to the max: it should ring with laughter and the sound of many feet. Sagamore has a heartbeat, which I became more aware of during my recent health scares. I feel the house has a soul.

I looked at the dusty work diaries, kept meticulously by Annie. It was difficult to see how I had fitted everything in. After cabaret in Glasgow, Manchester, Sheffield or wherever, I'd commute by train back to London to record TV commercial jingles, then head north again, only to return south two days later to record a radio or TV show, and go back to the north for more cabaret. When I did the summer cabaret season I still had to commute to London for recordings. A good example is mid-1965 to late 1966 when I released eight singles, featured in four TV variety shows, completed five television commercials and performed in over two hundred cabaret shows – all this before I'd had a significant hit record. At this time, while I was doing mostly radio, I appeared with the likes of Cliff Richard, The Beatles, Jerry and the Pacemakers and Americans Andy Williams, Roger Miller, Gene Pitney and Neil Sedaka on live shows during the day, and was on stage in (for example) Manchester in the evening, more often than not doubling at another venue by midnight. I had no way of knowing, but I eventually paid the price for all this.

In 1956, around the time I left the army and arrived in London to make my way as a professional singer, a German film entitled *Die Trapp-Familie* (*The Trapp Family*) made its debut. This and a sequel, *Die Trapp-Familie in Amerika*, were seen by the director Vincent Donehue, who thought they would make a fabulous musical – to feature his friend Mary Martin. Initially, and inexplicably given Mary's musical connections, it was seen as a non-musical play that would feature some songs from the Trapp family repertoire. Fortunately for her, for me and without doubt for lovers of musicals the world over, Leland Hayward and Mary Martin's husband Richard Halliday decided to commission Rodgers and Hammerstein to write new songs . . . and the rest, as they say, is history.

I first became aware of *The Sound Of Music* through the musical press. It wasn't just the trade press that extolled its virtues. '*Sound Of Music* Lights Up Broadway' one headline read: it was 1959 and the show had just opened in America. Annie and I were already sufficiently hooked to keep an eye out for its arrival in the UK. We didn't have long to wait, as it opened in London's West End in 1961. We were there for the opening night. I don't remember a great deal about it if I'm honest. It's not that I didn't enjoy it, and I was most impressed by the musical score, but nothing jumped out at me shouting 'I'm a hit record'. But when the film came out in 1965, with all the razzmatazz that goes with a musical marvel, a strange thing began to happen. As I said, I was almost constantly on tour in cabaret on both the theatre and club circuit, and in those days the working men's clubs (WMCs) were a prolific source of top-class entertainment. Television and popular legend frequently depict this, with the Wheeltappers and Shunters Social Club, for example. The clubs were wealthy back then, and could afford the best entertainment available. Tom Jones and Shirley Bassey are examples of those who worked in social clubs, and committees threw the best 'turns' at their members for decades. Little wonder they were fussy and hard to play to from an entertainer's point of view. There are thousands of stories still told to this day.

It was while I was working at some of these wonderful (and scary) establishments that people began to ask if I would sing 'Edelweiss' from *The Sound of Music*. Had it been a one-off request I probably wouldn't have thought much about it, but it seemed to be happening every week. When I got back to London I popped in to see Bob Barrett, my record producer at Columbia, and told him about all these requests. When I asked what he thought, his opinion was pretty much the same as mine: it was hard to imagine how we could make a recording with any aspirations of chart success. I went on my way, and life trundled on. Then six months later the phone rang, and it was Bob. 'That song you were asking me about. Well, it's in the Irish charts and I think we should do it after all.'

Even then nothing happened immediately; then out of the blue Bob called to say that the studio was booked, together with the Johnny Arthey Orchestra and the Eddie Lester Singers – so would I come in to record it the following week.

In retrospect, I don't think I anticipated success as the day of the session approached, with no premonitions that this might be the big one. However, there were two subsequent events that with hindsight might indicate that some things are meant to be.

Bob booked the Abbey Road Studios, made famous by the classic picture of The Beatles walking single file across the zebra crossing. On a beautiful summer's day in July 1966 Johnny's orchestra, together with Eddie's singers, presented a formidable line-up to record a song with me. I had worked in the studios many times before and had done hundreds of recordings over the years; frankly I saw this as just another session. The score seemed distinctly uninteresting. I looked through it several times, hoping for some kind of guidance or instruction, divine or otherwise, but nothing was forthcoming. Then Bob shouted, 'OK . . . let's take a run through.' In the absence of any other ideas I decided to stand there, sing it like a choirboy and see what happened. Then something strange occurred. The melody was familiar to us all, but as the first few bars sounded in my earphones and the alp horn resonated almost every hair on my body seemed to stand on end, and I shivered involuntarily. If you listen to the original recording you'll hear that there are no gimmicks, no special effects, just an easy, almost reverent, respectful production of a lovely song. We finished with surprisingly few takes, and it all ended with everyone peacefully going their various ways.

A week later Bob Barrett rang me to say that one of Columbia's senior executives felt there was something missing at the beginning, and could we look at that section again. Bob and I obediently got together with the engineers and I hummed, perhaps even breathed, some harmony into the intro, and we sent it back to the top man – not really knowing what else to do. He came back with, 'Great! That's just what it needed,' and I for one breathed a huge sigh of relief.

That really should have been the end of my beginning with 'Edelweiss', but in a little town in South Wales a lady called Gwen Owen was about to have a prayer answered. Destiny was about to take an amazing ace from its pack. The very next morning I was awakened by the shrill ring of the telephone on what was intended to be a rare day off. I don't know why, but I knew it was Bob Barrett.

'You'll never believe it, but we've got nothing in the tin trunk to put on the flipside of Edelweiss.' His voice had a touch of desperation which made me sit up and take notice. 'Have you got any ideas?'

The tin trunk was a trade expression to describe the store of recordings we kept for such times as these. Nothing immediately came to mind, but I told him to let me think about it.

Just then Annie came into our bedroom with a mug of tea, and told me she'd forgotton to mention that one of the national women's magazines had been on the telephone the evening before, wanting to speak to me about a song competition.

When I rang back later in the morning, a charming lady explained that they had been asking their readers to submit original song lyrics. The competition winner would have the music written by a famous singer, and the song would be released as the flipside of his next record release. Copyright law makes it clear that the record royalties for both sides are split equally between all writers, so it was common practice to try and get your own composition on the flip because it could be a potential money-spinner. Obviously the magazine must have done some deal to make it good for the artist who was about to give away some of his earnings, but when she told me the prize had been awarded and was about to be released I wondered why she wanted to speak to me.

She went on to explain that the lyric which had come second was her own personal favourite. As I was her favourite singer, she thought she'd ask if I'd take a look at it. Her charm won the day and, Bob's despair being still fresh in my mind, I told her to send it over. It arrived promptly, I liked it and had little trouble putting music to it. The writer Gwen Owen was thoroughly likeable and unpretentious, and her lyric for 'A Woman Needs Love' became the flipside to 'Edelweiss'.

It was the custom for recording artistes with new releases to ring up their record producers to get the latest sales figures. These were the provisional placings for the following weekend's chart, and naturally enough we all champed at the bit, wondering if we were going to enter the top ten. Usually we got the placings a day early. I'm quite sure that every recording artist will have a different perspective on this, as the industry has a thousand success stories and tens of thousands of the other sort, but the thrill of achieving a best-selling record has to be up there with the ultimate highs. A footballer described scoring a goal in front of fifty thousand people as being better than an orgasm, and a lottery winner described the worries of the world draining out like a waterfall of joy . . . and the news of a hit record, believe me, is up there with the best of 'em.

When 'Edelweiss' was released I rang Bob Barrett as I usually did on a Monday morning, to ask for sales figures. I'd experienced a cross section of responses in my career, varying from 'Sorry, Vince, nothing to report' to 'Twenty-five copies this week and the amazing 'Quite good, dear boy, three hundred and seventy'. I didn't expect anything to the contrary this time: it was a routine weekly event, and I was doodling, my mind on a forthcoming train journey to Scotland. 'Anything to report, Bob?'

'Are you sitting comfortably?'

I felt an abrupt sensation of unease, and sank into a chair by the phone. My record sales had been slowly rising since 'River's Run Dry', and 'Take Me To Your Heart Again' had stayed in the charts long after all expectation. The thought of sinking back to the misery of 'Sorry, only ten copies, Vince' was demoralising in the extreme. 'Yeah, I'm sitting down,' I said resignedly.

Bob's voice was deliberate. 'Twenty six thousand, four hundred and seventy five . . . and rising so fast that the record manufacturers have been caught with their trousers down!'

I was dumbstruck. A feeling of elation swept over me. I heard myself speaking calm words to him before replacing the receiver.

'My God! I've made it!'

The impact of this success began to make itself felt almost at once. My agent Dave Forrester of Forrester George was inundated with offers of work on the cabaret circuit, and my telephone took on a life of its own. One of the calls cemented my arrival at the very pinnacle of the industry, perhaps even more so than having a hit record. When I picked up the phone a voice said, 'This is Alec Fine, head of ATV. Would you like to appear on *Sunday Night at the London Palladium* with Jack Benny?' Annie and I had just moved into a new house at Roehampton (in south-west London). It needed a great deal of work: none of the services worked properly, and there was a hole in the roof under which I had placed a chamber pot to catch the rain. As Alec offered me an opportunity that every entertainer in the business would give their eye teeth for, I was holding the phone in one hand and a potty in the other!

The variety industry has disappeared now, and some readers

may not understand the honour and glory associated with such a distinction. The Palladium was one thing, but with Jack Benny: that was something else. It may suffice to record the comment made by agent Kenneth Earle, half of Earle and Vaughan – one of the most successful comedy vocal acts of the '50s. When he and his partner walked on stage at their next venue after appearing on *Sunday Night at the London Palladium*, they received a standing ovation before they uttered a word – on the strength of that TV appearance. For my part I would liken it to winning *Strictly Come Dancing* and *The X-Factor* on the same day.

The fact that I was to be on with Jack Benny took the whole experience into orbit. Benny was one of America's best-loved comedy entertainers, and probably more famous than any other variety professional in the English-speaking world. I was in complete awe of him, revering his slow, deliberate style and compulsive dry humour. I'd have walked from Roehampton to the Palladium on my knees to appear with him.

Not that I said any of this to Alec Fine, of course. I thanked him courteously, said I would be honoured to appear, and put the pot back under the leak in the roof.

This particular *Sunday Night at the London Palladium* was in fact the *Jack Benny Show* by any other name, and it was quite a coup for ATV. The full bill was Benny as compère and star, Max Bygraves, Kiki Dee, Dusty Springfield and me, and although by this time I'd been around for quite a few years I was to a large extent the new kid on the block. Because of this, Benny decided to use me as the 'new kid' in a wise-cracking sketch. This had me receiving advice from the great man, then precociously offering him advice regarding his famous slow delivery. The audience loved it, and it stretched my four minute spot to twelve minutes . . . in front of 24 million people!

'Edelweiss' went on to earn me a silver disc, and opened doors that are available to only a privileged minority. Not only are there agents who'll only consider representing artistes who've had a hit record, but there are venues that automatically accept you if you've had one: it gives you membership to a very exclusive club.

Furthermore, it narrows the Atlantic gap, and brings the fame that every singer craves – as an alcoholic yearns for a drink.

I'd worked hard and earned extremely well for a considerable time, but the fame that 'Edelweiss' brought ' and the way my performance fees increased was mind-blowing. There were adjustments to make not only in our private lives but also in the way I was received as an entertainer. I was often embarrassed by the way ordinary people reacted to me. Humbled by their attention, I constantly tried to dispel the myths that fame seems to create. I'd like to think that I've remained one of the people, and have never forgotten my roots.

Some years later an episode occurred that put fame and success into perspective like no other, and I feel emotional whenever it comes to mind. Gwen Owen, who wrote the lyrics for 'A Woman Needs Love', stayed in touch and we exchanged telephone calls for many years. One Sunday evening Annie was on the phone to her while I half-watched television in the background. I was distracted by Annie's expression, and as I watched tears began to run down her face. When the conversation ended, she turned to me. 'Gwen's just told me that when she wrote her lyric for you she had financial problems and a severely disabled daughter. The royalties from "Edelweiss" provided medical treatment and her daughter's special education, and completely changed their lives. Vince, she told me that "Edelweiss" really did help her to climb every mountain.'

CHAPTER NINE

Annie, Can You Spare A Dime?

'Edelweiss' not only changed Gwen and her daughter's lives, but it also changed ours. My diary was already full, with cabaret commitments, TV commercial recordings, demo recordings for music publishers and radio or television appearances; but suddenly, overnight, my fees doubled, trebled and then went through the roof! The phone line from Dave Forrester at the Forrester George office was red hot for weeks as 'Edelweiss' climbed and climbed the charts.

Soon after 'Edelweiss' entered the charts, Dave shifted a whole section of engagements to accommodate a long seasonal run in *Cinderella* at the Palace Theatre in Manchester. I shared the top billing with Des O'Connor and the cast included comedians Jack Douglas and Joe Black, and Pippa Steel, the prettiest little Cinders you ever saw. Pippa went on to star in two successful vampire movies and had a whole host of television roles, ranging from *Blake's 7*, *The Young Winston* and *Public Eye* to *Oh! What A Lovely War*, *Z-Cars* and *Department S*. Another character is worth mentioning: the beautiful Tanya and her master, whose name escapes me. Tanya was an Indian elephant trained to do all sorts of things, which were specially adapted for the show. Annie took an immediate shine to Tanya and adored her perhaps only slightly less than the elephant did Annie, especially after Annie had discovered Tanya's soft spot for marshmallows. The trouble was the effect that the marshmallows had on her . . . it's bad enough if you have a pet dog that wants to do a poo, but when an elephant wants to do one . . . the result was huge, and everywhere! Annie withdrew the treats at once, despite frequent and persistent attentions, and the handler never found out her guilty secret. Elephants, of course, never forget and thereafter Tanya's trunk often strayed waywardly at the sound of sweet papers.

With 'Edelweiss' flying high, the song was introduced into the pantomime, in which I played Prince Charming to Pippa's Cinders – although it wasn't staged quite as well as Columbia Records would have liked, had they had a say in it. Cinders was asleep and dreaming about her prince, while I sang from behind a sheet of gauze. Although it was effective from a production point of view, it didn't do much to promote the record. Not that it needed much help, though: *The Sound Of Music* had popularised the song, and the public were longing for a romantic version of it – a fact that seemed to have gone unnoticed by everyone except me and Bob Barrett.

I was fondly looking back at this particular era and chatting with a like-minded soul when Annie took a call from Jane Apperley's office. My results were through and could I go and see her. 'There's nothing to worry about unduly,' Annie was told, but I was still suspicious of my condition and perhaps of Annie too. Obviously it was no good telling someone to keep bad news from you and then criticising them for doing so, but the problem with such an arrangement was that you tended to expect the worst.

'I've decided I want the truth from the hospital in future,' I said to Annie. 'Sorry to mess you about.'

'That's OK,' she responded, only half-listening.

'I'm going for a swim with Doris,' I added sarcastically.

'OK,' she replied.

As I headed for the river bank, I wondered if my favourite duck would be there. She'd been absent since her drunken session in the orchard, and few of the others had shown up for several days afterwards. Even now only one or two drifted across the water to where I stood. I wondered if ducks could get cirrhosis of the liver, or perhaps she'd been so inebriated that she'd had an accident with a boat ... could ducks drown? I began to feel a bit guilty for deserting her in her hour of need. Should I have taken her back to the house? Should I have let her sleep it off in the shed? I'd unburdened so many of my problems on her, talking nonsense partly through despair and then through panic, worry and anxiety. 'Bloody coward that you are!' I shouted out loud.

Quack! Quack! There was a flurry of spray from mid-stream and a blur of movement as a lone duck took off, heading straight for me. Doris landed a yard or so away from me, as scruffy as ever – but to me she was beautiful. 'You bloody cow bag,' I said with a smile and a lump in my throat. 'Where the hell have you been?'

She was as patient as ever, and sat there long after the food had disappeared listening to my ramblings. I wasn't altogether sure what she made of me, but I found it helpful to tell her my innermost secrets, worries and fears. I wondered how close she'd let me get, so I picked up a stray piece of bread and walked slowly towards her, careful not to make any sudden movement. I held it out but she made no effort to take it. When I moved in closer there was still no interest, so I pushed it until it touched her beak. I could swear she shook her head; Doris had eaten her fill.

I sat down and started to tell her that I had another appointment with Jane Apperley, but she didn't seem to want to hear about hospitals and got up and waddled back to the river. 'Cheerio,' I said, 'and be careful.'

I watched fascinated as she swam slowly towards the other side of the river, but as usual her pace slowed two thirds of the way across, and she allowed herself to drift downstream with the current until she was out of sight.

I walked back to the house, and my thoughts reverted to the '60s and 'Edelweiss'. I never set out to be a pop singer in the traditional sense: I strived to get a hit record so I'd gain credibility, which would give me a bigger stage for my cabaret floor show. I put a great deal of thought and design into my stage act and it always had a theme. The bigger the hit, the bigger the venue, the bigger the stage, the more effective the theme ... and hits don't come much bigger than

'Edelweiss'. But it seems to me there's a balance of payments. A lucky break or a splendid piece of luck is always balanced with a downside. As well as the gauze hiding me from plugging my hit at the panto, Des O'Connor released a little song called 'Careless Hands' while he was appearing with me in Manchester, which immediately put us on an equal footing – just to remind me that I wasn't the only recording artiste with a hit. Des is one of the nice guys, and I was delighted for him.

As I walked back into the house I spotted a magazine on a table in the hallway. On the cover was a picture of several classic cars, one of them a 1960s Vauxhall Cresta. I'd owned one, and smiled as I recalled the circumstances in which it was sold. It was at the time of *Cinderella* in Manchester and I'd bought it new. Although I did most of my commuting by train and tube, a car was useful when public transport wasn't feasible. I can't even remember why I chose the Cresta, except that it was colourful and flashy with an American style. Such is youth!

One day, on my way to the theatre for a matinée, I passed a second-hand car showroom which I usually glanced at on my way past. On this occasion, centre-stage in all its glory, there was a magnificent 1950s Bentley. I fell in love immediately. Walking round the white apparition, I saw what I wanted to see – ignoring the rust around the doors and the uneven paintwork. A typically flash car salesman promptly pointed out that as a 'pop star' (as he described me) I needed a status symbol. After all, he wanted next to nothing for it! I told him I'd have to discuss it with the wife, and then drove to the theatre thinking only of the magnificence of the marque, and not of Flash Harry's example.

'Annie!' I exclaimed, when I got back to the house we were renting in Styal, just outside the city. 'There's something I really want.' I proceeded to describe the illusion with all the splendour of my imaginings, pointing out that I rarely bought anything just for me, and I'd never wanted anything so much since I'd wanted to get out of the coalmines.

Annie stood quietly, and when I finished she took a deep breath. 'Sorry, Vince ... we haven't got any money.'

I'd looked at her incredulously, my mouth opening and closing like a goldfish. Annie's job was managing the money, I was too busy, and was privately pleased that she seemed to enjoy it. Thoughts of how she could have spent everything we'd earned swept through my mind. Did she have an addiction? Was she a shopaholic? Had we been stitched up by somebody?

'Sit down, darling,' she said calmly. 'You see, Vince, I've been investing our money in property. We've got a house in East Acton, and we're about to buy another nearby.'

'Property . . .' I said pathetically, as if it was a commodity unknown to me.

'Yes . . . you know, bricks and mortar.' I detected a slight sarcasm but her expression didn't change. 'You see, singers don't get pensions and we've got absolutely no idea how long your popularity will last. We've got to make arrangements accordingly. I thought property was the best bet. You do agree, don't you, darling?'

'Yes,' I muttered, wondering if we had enough cash left to go to the Chinese restaurant for a meal. 'I'll have to tell Flash I've changed my mind,' I added miserably.

'Who's Flash?'

'Don't ask.' My voice had faded and I was deep in thought.

'Not the lovely man selling the Bentley, perchance?' Annie had a glint in her eye.

'No, of course not. What do you think about me doing a part exchange for the Vauxhall?'

'Do what you like, Vince. Cars are your department.'

'Yes, of course.' I squinted at my property investor wife, who was looking through a mass of paperwork that seemed to contain pictures of more houses.

Flash Harry was pleased to see me back, although it has to be said that the smile dropped when I told him I'd got no money. 'How about a part exchange for my new Vauxhall?' I asked pathetically, seeing my Bentley aspirations disappear.

'It'll have to be one for one,' he said quickly.

'But what about the rust?' I asked, pointing at the bottom of the Bentley's doors.

'I'll throw that in,' was his nonchalant reply, 'and that's my final offer.'

He knew he'd hooked a fish. 'OK, deal,' I confirmed. Less than an hour later I drove away my illusion.

I have to say Annie hated what she describes to this day as 'that vulgar thing', but I loved it, for a while anyway. Predictably it cost so much in repairs that I was forced to change it a year or so later. We live and learn.

A few days after I'd bought the Bentley, Annie sat me down and told me to clear my mind of musical arrangements, orchestrations, stage routines and recording sessions for long enough to hear about her property plans. She reminded me of two friends, Maria and Dennis, who'd been close to her in Acton. Maria had made Annie's wedding dress and Dennis was a master carpenter. 'They've emigrated to New Zealand now, but it nearly didn't happen. You see, they sold everything bar the kitchen sink and were sailing on the Monday morning, but the Friday before the people who were buying their house pulled out. Can you imagine the fix they were in? All their possessions were in transit and the house was completely empty . . . and she made my wedding dress for nothing!' Annie added, too quickly.

There was silence for a moment or two while I put it all together. 'So . . . you bought their house as a favour because she made your wedding dress?'

'Yes – and there's not a scrap of rust on it anywhere,' she said pointedly.

I switched on the television and sat down to watch nothing in particular, still thinking affectionately of the days of yore, and musing over one memory that cast a dark shadow. Pippa Steel, who had charmed so many children, tantalised grown-ups in more than one pantomime, and stunned a generation all too briefly with her beauty on film and television, tragically died from cancer when she was too young.

CHAPTER TEN

Murder Most Foul

Margaret Reynolds and Diane Tift, aged six and five respectively, were two delightful little girls. Margaret disappeared on her way to school on 8 September 1965, and hundreds of local people helped in a massive search that yielded nothing. Three months later Diane was playing near her home in Bloxwich, and she too mysteriously disappeared.

In January 1966 a workman discovered the body of a child in a field near Cannock Chase, and when the forensic team moved the lifeless form for further examination it was to discover a second child beneath. The search for Margaret and Diane was over. Six months later ten-year-old Jane Taylor went for a ride on her bicycle in the vicinity of Cannock Chase, and was never seen again.

Towards the end of the year Raymond Leslie Morris was accused of taking two young girls to his home, where he undressed them. As neither child could corroborate the other's testimony because they were taken to separate rooms, charges were eventually dropped.

On 19 August 1967 seven-year-old Christine Darby was playing with some friends in Walsall when a car pulled up nearby and the door opened. The smiling male driver asked for directions to a local area, and inexplicably Christine climbed into the car – which immediately sped off in the opposite direction. A week later her body was found in a field: she had been seriously assaulted and strangled.

Witness descriptions of the car led detectives to interview a number of local men, and attention fell on Raymond Morris as a result of his being accused in the molestation charges. Unfortunately his wife gave him a perfect alibi, saying that he had been shopping with her whenChristine had been murdered, so reluctantly the police had to drop their line of inquiry.

Shortly afterwards Morris tried to abduct ten-year-old Margaret Aulton, but the attempt was foiled. A neighbour took down his car's registration number and he was arrested. When the police searched his home they discovered pornographic photographs of his niece, which prompted his wife to admit to the police that she'd fabricated his shopping alibi. Morris was subsequently sentenced to life imprisonment. Detective Chief Superintendent Pat Molloy, one of the leading officers on the case, said he had no doubt that Morris was connected to other murders. The Cannock Chase murders and abductions of little girls had gone on for four years, and only stopped after Morris was arrested.

During the summer of 1969, in the middle of one of the most exhausting years of my entire career, Annie presented me as usual with the monthly pile of fan mail laid out in orderly fashion, with pictures ready to sign. As I ploughed through the arduous but necessary ritual, a small envelope dropped from the pile: it had somehow been missed. I absent-mindedly slit it open and pulled out a single sheet of paper, to read the first of many words from my lover Suzie . . . or so she called herself.

> *Dearest darling Vince,*
> *Our first night together was unforgettable and the*
> *memory of your yellow satin pyjamas next to my baby*
> *doll nightie will live in my mind forever.*
> *I am forever yours*
> *Suzie*
> *X*

It brought a smile to my face. An acquaintance of mine who was a press officer once told me that with my Mr Clean image I was a publicist's nightmare. 'If you'd slept your way round the world with a few tasty names, I could get you in every paper and magazine in creation,' he said, with a hopeful expression on his face. Sadly for him I was just as my image suggested, and given the many unhappy souls I knew in the business who'd lived as he would have liked me to have done I had no regrets.

I passed the letter over to Annie and asked how she thought I'd managed to fit the liaison into my schedule, and she replied by tossing it onto the fire. It would have been so nice had it ended there.

Less than a week later another immediately identifiable envelope arrived, the enclosed letter describing the increased intensity of Suzie's and my romance. More arrived, and our amusement began to change to alarm – particularly when she made reference to details she couldn't have been privy to without some knowledge of my movements. Then she informed me she was pregnant.

A week or so passed without communication from Suzie, then one morning I was breakfasting early before catching a plane to Glasgow when I spotted her familiar envelope. It was thicker than usual, and I opened it as if I expected something to jump out and bite me . . . and in a way it did.

This was the week of the arrest of Raymond Morris, and the papers were full of reports of the murders. Suzie's letter was brief:

> *I know it was you who did it.*
> *Suzie*

Attached to her note was a clipping from a tabloid newspaper. In it was a picture of Morris with a coat draped over his head as he was taken from a police vehicle into court for his murder trial. Approximately where his head would have been was a newspaper picture of mine, neatly cut out and pasted onto Morris's body. A wave of nausea swept over me. It was so powerful that I retched.

During the subsequent weeks more letters followed, and we decided to involve the police. At first they were reluctant as there was nothing on the outside of the letters that could offend the public; this was how the law stood at the time. I was extremely angry and said so. Then Suzie made a mistake. She sent me a parcel which she had registered for safe delivery, and of course if mail is registered the sender's name and address is retained by the post office. Finally cooperating fully, thanks to the intensity and serious nature of Suzie's actions, the police set off to arrest the perpetrator; but there was to be a shock in store. Suzie wasn't Suzie at all. Neither was she operating, as I'd imagined, from a dingy inner city flat. She lived in a comfortable home in Lincolnshire with her loving parents. She was a mentally disturbed teenager.

Few things have terrified and disturbed me more than the events that led up to her arrest. Nothing has ever moved me more than the telephone call from her distraught parents, who apologised profusely for the suffering their daughter had caused. I doubt anyone will ever apologise to them for their plight and misery . . . not in this life anyway.

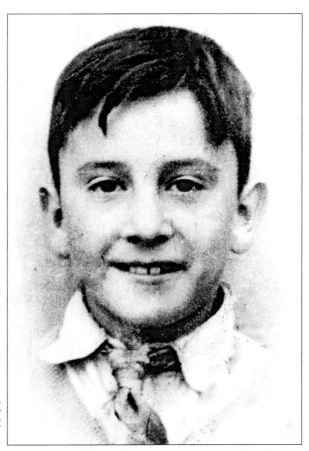

Who's this handsome young chap? Vince, aged about seven.

Vince's first ever appearance on stage – where it all began. Not *The X Factor*, but winning a talent show at the Prospect pub in Margate, 1949 or 1950.

Vince with the Band of the Royal Corps of Signals, 1954.

The Four Others: Vince, Bobby Blaine, Val Williams and Len Beadle. Vince and Len went on to form The Raindrops.

Annie and Vince, 4 June 1959. And they said it wouldn't last!

Vince (on the left) and The Raindrops.

The Raindrops, early '60s. Left to right: Vince, Len Beadle, Jackie Lee and Johnny Worth.

Annie meets The Raindrops!

Vince, Len Beadle, Jackie and Brian Adams (replacing Johnny Worth) with Tommy Steele, Coventry Theatre, 1962.

Vince at the Rio Music Festival , 1971 – where he won the public vote for most popular singer.

Vince and son Athol, 1973.

With Dilys Laye as Ivor Novello's mother in *My Dearest Ivor*.

Vince and Suzi Quatro with Barbara Cartland on their lunchtime TV chat show, *Gas Street*.

Vince at the Palladium.

A proud moment. Vince meets the Queen Mother at the Royal Variety Show, Drury Lane Theatre.

Dinner at Sagamore: Vince, wife Annie and great friend and mentor
Cliff Adams.

Vince, Cliff Adams and long-time friend and brilliant painter Bill Mundy –
whose picture graces the cover of this book.

Playing Ivor Novello in a scene from *King's Rhapsody* during the record-breaking run of *My Dearest Ivor:* Sonning, late 1980s.

Another number from *My Dearest Ivor*, with the great Dilys Laye as Ivor's 'Mam' and the delightful Louise English, one time Hill's Angel and top West End star.

With Lulu at the Conservative rally at Wembley. Jerry Herman had given permission for the lyrics of his song to be changed to 'Hello Maggie'.

Bill and Vince check early versions of the cover picture.

'Can you taste what it is yet?' Rolf loves Indian food.

'How does it go again, Rolf?'

Vince and the other love of his life: his beloved Teddy.

Vince, Doris and friends.

What was that tune?

The captain stocks up for an afternoon on the river!

CHAPTER ELEVEN

Those Who Love And Those Who Hate

My appointment with Jane Apperley was three weeks hence and the fact that it wasn't given the same priority as the previous consultations suggested to me that I could delay the last rites. I smiled, and was glad I could. I didn't have an accurate prognosis but I was definitely more philosophical than before.

I reflected briefly on the Suzie saga, and the downside of other aspects of the trappings of success. As an example . . . Annie did very well with her foray into the property business, but things are not always as they seem. The small property in East Acton was in outstanding condition and needed not a penny spent on it, so we rented it out to four nurses. A little over a year later their standing order was cancelled, so we decided to visit them at the house. The sight that met our eyes was devastating.

The remains of an old motorcycle lay in the front room. Someone had obviously been working on it, leaving oil stains everywhere. The kitchen had been desecrated. The bathroom and bedrooms were scenes of total destruction, and it causes me acute embarrassment to have to describe them even to this day. There were used sanitary towels in the bath and on the bathroom and bedroom floors, and used condoms in two of the beds. Food had been left on plates and on the floors, attracting flies and maggots. There was an indescribable smell of filth and decay. Annie burst into tears, and I dragged her out into the fresh air. It is to her great credit that she returned and fumigated and cleaned the entire place herself, replacing all the carpets and damaged fittings while I was appearing in another run at The Talk of the Town. Needless to say we sold the house shortly afterwards.

Annie's next purchase was the Roehampton house which, while intended to be our new home, was somewhat grander than we required. It was her idea to re-design and refurbish it completely, then make a profit by selling quickly. That it was run down and had that pesky leaking roof only increased its potential. Unfortunately things didn't quite go according to plan.

I was working away, recording Mike and Bernie Winters' TV show, and Annie was at home, holding the fort and liaising with solicitors and estate agents in order to push the sale through. It was Easter week, and although contracts had been exchanged it looked doubtful that completion would take place before the holiday. Then Annie was told late on the Thursday afternoon that the money had arrived, and the house was ours. Owing to the Easter holiday, and as a result of our oversight, the house insurance wasn't in place. Naturally enough, despite our being separated by a couple of hundred miles, a little thing like no insurance for two days wasn't going to spoil our excitement at the thought of this beautiful house, and our spirits were as high as they could possibly be. Imagine our shock three days later when Annie had a call from the police to tell us that our new house had been seriously damaged by fire. Four houses had been torched by vandals on the same night, and ours was the only one still standing.

I returned home the following day to find Annie in a mess. She was distraught at the fire damage, indignant because it was an act of arson, and blaming herself, at least in part, for the lack of insurance. I'd insisted that she waited for me to return before she went to see the damage, and we decided to drive over immediately. The sight that met our eyes was dreadful.

The house had been owned for many years by a General Munro, who had been Commander-in-Chief of the Mediterranean Expeditionary Force (in which role he led the evacuation of Gallipoli in 1915) and Commander-in-Chief of the Indian Army. The old man had died in 1929, but when we purchased the property in a probate sale some of his belongings still remained. Among them were dozens of reels of film of his many foreign trips and wartime adventures, which were fascinating and no doubt extremely valuable. We had carefully packed them up in a large trunk and asked his lawyers to remove them for safe keeping.

The sight that greeted us was one of massive destruction. There had evidently been a gang of vandals. Extensive damage had been done to fittings, and they had urinated and defecated in several rooms, smearing the result over walls and floors. In a calculating fashion, they had turned the keys in all the doors, so they could not be shut to contain the fire if it were discovered in time. Then they had soaked in petrol the curtains they had torn down, poured the remainder of the two cans they had brought with them throughout the house, and torched it. The valuable records of General Munro's life and times were destroyed, and where the trunk had lain there were two massive holes burned through the beautiful oak floors.

We stood in silence, surveying the desecration. Tears streamed down Annie's face and I swallowed hard, She clenched her fists, then spluttered indignantly, 'If I could get hold of them I'd cut their arms off! Not only have we got to clean it up ourselves, we've got to pay for the bloody repairs . . . so let's bloody get on with it!' Annie was angry!

If any good could possibly come from such an orgy of destruction, it was that the whole house had to be refurbished from top to bottom. This was a challenge that Annie relished, and after overcoming her shock she set about it with a will. Everything went according to plan. Annie had taken a bridging loan, which bought us some time, and I never ceased to be amazed at her skill.

Finally the great day arrived and at long last we moved in. To Annie's great credit, the results were so good that the house was featured in the magazines *Ideal Homes* and *Homes and Gardens*.

After 'Edelweiss', the follow-up 'Roses of Picardy' and my first album, we enjoyed the fan mail and accolades, but were also greatly amused by the detractors. Being a member of the old school, I'd learnt my craft working with some of the best professionals in the business, I was a regular on the northern club circuit and was a radio and TV veteran by the time I had my first hit, so I had the greatest of respect for public opinion. After all, the public decided the fate of folk like me, and just as I did my best to be magnanimous when things were going well, I made sure I was equally gracious when the cookie crumbled the other way. I always remember some old timer saying to me, 'Be nice on the way up, son, and maybe they'll be nice to you when you're on the way down.'

So it was that Annie and I read the letters page in the music press, particularly the *New Musical Express* (*NME*) and the *Melody Maker*, and howl at some of the comments that would have mortified people who took themselves too seriously. For example, Kevin Tunstall from London N19 wrote, 'I am astounded that Vince Hill's "Roses of Picardy" is in the Melody Maker Pop Charts, can't someone ban it?' Pete Townshend of The Who is quoted as saying, 'I'll eat my hat if Edelweiss gets into the charts.' Chas Chandler of The Animals declared, 'When crap like that gets into the charts it's time for me to leave the country!' I had the pleasure of meeting Ray Davies of The Kinks, who told me that when they were doing the clubs little old ladies used to ask them to play 'Roses of Picardy'. He said they never did it, and admitted that this was because it had too many chords! I doubt Pete Townshend ate his hat, but Chas Chandler certainly left for America shortly afterwards. And Ray was just having fun, because he's a superb musician and composer, and producer of some fabulous music.

Some fans are incredibly devoted, and Molly Hallgarth has got to be up there with the best of them. She managed to get herself into the *Guinness Book of Records* for having 227 requests played on local radio, and most of them were to hear my songs. Truly amazing!

Soon after moving to Roehampton I was working in pantomime at the Lyceum in Sheffield, playing the title role in *Dick Whittington*, when I received a call from producer Stewart Morris to ask if I would appear on the Rolf Harris Show. 'I want you to do "Soliloquy" from *Carousel*,' he said simply.

'Soliloquy', sometimes referred to as 'My Boy Bill', is very famous, but the musical score is twenty pages long – and a huge ask to perform live in front of God alone knows how many million people, especially if you've got my stage nerves. I estimated that it would take at least seven minutes, and I'd have to learn it as it wasn't in my repertoire. The answer was yes, of course, of that there was no doubt – so I thought of the coal mines and thanked Stewart for thinking of me. Then the fun started. Every night in Sheffield, right up to the eve of the *Rolf Harris Show*, I could be found in all sorts of obscure places at the Lyceum, singing away at my section of *Carousel* dressed as Dick Whittington!

As soon as I arrived at the television studios I grabbed Stewart Morris and suggested I should record the whole thing, because of its length and complexity and the obvious risk of error. 'If I cock it up, I can't la-la-la my bloody way around the "Soliloquy",' I said in desperation.

Stewart considered my request for about half a second. 'No chance. I want to see the fear in your eyes.'

To say it was a success is an understatement. The fan mail was huge, and the performance is still commented on to this day, which I find astonishing. Recently a pal rang me quite late and told me to turn to one of the Sky channels, which was doing a re-run of the *Rolf Harris Show* that I was on. I watched it intrigued, scrutinising every muscle in an attempt to spot the terror I'd experienced, and was so relieved when I could see nothing – as if it really mattered so many years after the event. Surprise, surprise, there were several e-mails sent to my website from those who appreciated seeing the performance again.

Rolf Harris has remained a close friend ever since. From the many occasions on which he came to dinner I remember one evening in particular. He arrived with a reel to reel tape recorder, explaining that an old mate from Oz had sent him a song and because of my musical background he'd like my opinion. He plugged it in and pressed the play button . . . 'Two little boys had two little toys, each had a wooden horse . . .'

'What d'ya think?'

'Record it straight away,' I said. 'It's a smash!'

CHAPTER TWELVE

Ern And The Turn

There were no radio announcements carrying sad tidings about friends, few traffic problems and no awkward silences on the way to Hammersmith Hospital. During the journey we joked about Doris Duck, and that she'd have to wait for her dinner. I was quite looking forward to seeing Jane Apperley again. I liked people who were good at what they did, and I was beginning to believe that thanks to her expert guidance chronic myeloid leukaemia wasn't going to kill me.

The room was packed but I managed to settle Annie into a comfortable seat, and walked confidently over to the receptionist, who I recognised immediately; she seemed to know me too. 'Looks busy today,' I remarked. 'Are we all seeing the same doctor?'

'You're seeing Dr Marin today, Mr Hill. He's running on time, so you shouldn't have to wait long.'

As she spoke I was shuffling through my hospital letters, which were all neatly clipped together, and for a split second I thought she was talking to another patient behind me. I turned round, but there was no-one there. As I turned back to the receptionist realisation dawned. 'Are you sure? I normally see Professor Apperley.'

The receptionist smiled the smile of a customer service professional. 'Today it's Dr Marin. He'll bring you up to date with your progress. I'm sure you'll like him.'

'Yes . . . of course . . . I'm, well . . . it's just that . . . yes, OK . . . thank you.'

I hurried back to Annie, and spoke too loudly. 'I'm not seeing Jane. It's some bloody stand-in – and you know what stand-ins do . . . they stand in,' I said inanely.

'He's not going to bloody sing to you, Vince. He's probably a consultant too. You don't really think you're going to get a medical student at this stage, do you? For heaven's sake sit down and relax.'

I began to calm down, and looked around to see if anyone had noticed my outburst. But there was no reaction: they were all too immersed in their own imminent deaths to notice me, I reasoned. 'Damn it, there I go again,' I said out loud, angry at my negative thoughts.

'What?'

'It's OK. I'm just getting maudlin again. I'm really sorry, I just can't get used to this being ill thing . . . and anyway, I don't feel ill until I get here!'

'Mr Hill, can you come through, please?' A nurse had come in without me noticing, and I raised my hand instinctively. She smiled and came over. 'We have to take a little blood first, but I expect you're getting used to that by now. It won't take many minutes.'

Her extremely courteous and professional approach kept my traumas to a minimum, and soon six phials of blood were taken away for testing. I admit that my thoughts drifted back to the memorable TV sketch in which Tony Hancock thought he was losing an armful. In no time at all the process was completed, and we found ourselves back in the crowded waiting room to await the test results.

Just a few minutes later the nurse returned, and we followed her once again. 'Have you met Dr Marin before?' she said amiably. I wasn't sure if she was making small talk or checking her records, but I shook my head, at the same time thinking how ridiculous it would be to ask how long he'd been out of medical school. But any doubts I had about my new doctor, a charming gentleman, were soon dispelled – although he had a very strong Spanish accent.

'Meester Heel, please sit down. I see you're a seenger. I remember some of your songs.'

'Oh, how nice . . .'

Dr Marin was on a roll. 'I'd like you to know I'm learning za cello . . . it's good for za relaxing.'

'As a matter of fact I'm taking guitar lessons. I'm not that good yet, though.'

'Perhaps we could get one of za nurses to play za drums, and we could 'ave za 'ospital trio! Now . . .'

When Dr Marin paused to tap his keyboard and scrutinise the screen, I quickly interrupted. 'I was a bit worried that my blood tests might be affected, so I haven't had any wine or alcohol of any sort for at least a week.'

He looked at me for a moment, apparently stunned. 'Goodness gracious, you mean not even a tiny drop with your dinner?' I shook my head. 'Well, zat's quite dredderful. You must 'ave za little drop, or what is life for?'

Dr David Marin proved to be another master at his craft. He explained my progress carefully, and how the medication had stabilised the leukaemia, emphasising that I was currently in remission. He made it clear that while nothing was set in stone, he was pleased, and would be even more so if I continued stable when I next visited him. I was beginning to see even more light at the end of the tunnel.

I pulled out of the car park into a stream of traffic joining the slow procession that led to the A40 heading out of London, occasionally looking at the faces of other travellers and wondering what ordeals they were coping with in their lives.

'Ernie's pulled out a million pound win for an old lady up north. I do hope it brings her happiness.' Annie was reading a newspaper she'd purchased at the hospital shop, and went on with a political story – but my thoughts had gone off at a tangent.

The 'Ernie' to which Annie referred was the sophisticated machine (an **E**lectronic **R**andom **N**umber **I**ndicator) that drew out winning premium bonds for the lucky few. To me, Ernie was Ernie Dunstall, my long-time musical director, close friend and confidant for a quarter of a century and in a way he was a sophisticated machine too. If I fed a musical theme or idea into his computer-like brain, it scrambled it all about and sent it back with added intricacies and elaborations: pure genius, delivered with a charm that computers don't possess. As a budding composer I frequently hummed him a tune that I had buzzing around in my head, then shoved the lyrics in front of him and said, 'Make me a silk purse out of this sow's ear.' And he always did. When we were touring I always introduced Ernie like this: 'Ladies and gentlemen, may I introduce my right-hand tonsil, guide and mentor – Ernie Dunstall.'

I first met Ernie in 1956 when I was singing with the Teddy Foster Band, and as a young starry-eyed singer I boggled at his skills, playfully telling him on many occasions that when I became a star I'd 'take him away from all this'. How prophetic that simple banter was. I used him on the odd gig along the way, and as my fortunes improved I paid him a retainer so he could put in a deputy if a booking clashed with something he already had in the book; but in 1968 Ernie joined me full time.

It was a partnership that lasted a quarter of a century, and without doubt we were the very best of friends – often referring to ourselves and Annie as the three musketeers. We were much younger then, of course, and there were so many experiences and adventures – especially when we were touring foreign parts – and as we chugged up the A40 I recalled some of them.

One event came immediately to mind. After a theatre booking somewhere in the north of England several star 'turns' went to elaborate ends to avoid hundreds of fans milling around the stage door area. I managed to miss out on this plan somehow, and walked straight through the stage door with Ernie into the waiting hordes. Fortunately there was some sort of barrier, but we still had to run the gauntlet of autograph hunters. I dutifully signed . . . and signed . . . and signed, with the expressionless Ernie standing behind me. Suddenly someone said to him, 'Are *you* anyone, mate?'

Quick as a flash he replied, 'No – not just at the moment!'

One of Ernie's favourite tales was about arriving at a Yorkshire working men's club, where he was acting as musical associate to the bandleader who was providing my backing. It was quite a large resident band with a huge local reputation. The keyboard player took one look at Ernie's orchestrations and I saw him shake his head, Ernie looked in my direction and, seeing my concern, walked over. 'He can't play this, because it hasn't got a picture on the front!' Sheet music was usually simply written with the top line depicting the melody line, the left hand in elementary form and the names of the chords along the bottom. For all the band's local reputation, anything more complicated than this wasn't on their agenda.

It's widely accepted that WMC backing bands were either fabulous or rubbish. I'd had several wonderful encounters with club musicians, and one worth recounting occurred in Yorkshire shortly before 'Edelweiss'. When I attended the customary band call before the show I produced Ernie's wonderful arrangement. The keyboard player took one look and exclaimed, 'Eh, lad . . . I can't play this . . . it's bin written by a chord maniac!'

The first tour that I did with Ernie abroad came about in a most unusual way. I'd been working with a female singer called Terri Scott, and during an after show chat one night she told me that she and her husband Dick Citroen were emigrating to Canada. Several months later I received a phone call from her asking if I would be interested in doing a series on Canadian TV. It transpired that my records were played widely on radio stations over there and I was something of a name. Dick, it appeared, was attempting to establish himself as a television producer and, armed with pictures and cuttings of *Stars and Garters*, he suggested to one of the stations that they should hire me for a similar variety series. Ernie and I flew over to meet the network executives and to discuss terms, and returned with a contract to record twenty-six half-hour family shows entitled *Vince Hill At The Club*.

A few months later Ernie and I returned to Canada, this time accompanied by Annie. We arrived at a beautiful detached mini-mansion provided for us on the outskirts of town, fresh and ready for work. However, we were in for a surprise. You often read how British television is the finest in the world, and if I ever needed an example of how productions in other countries can vary from ours I now had a perfect example. It proved to be quite a culture shock.

The whole thing was badly organised to the point of there being no organisation at all. Dick Citroen, who we had to thank for the contract, was so new to television that he looked to me and to Ernie to help with the production, a job which to all intents and purposes was as new to us as it was to him. We knew that the producer was supposed to be head of the production team, with an assistant who was a fully competent TV person who'd come through the ranks, having served in most if not all departments on the way. On his other side there would be a writer, also with assistant, responsible for a professional script to be delivered on demand. The assistant producer would have a crew of personnel with designated responsibilities. The simple fact, though, was that we had Dick Citroen – a perfectly nice chap but a 'wannabe', a versatile comic called Dave Armour, Ernie and me. Nick Olchowey, a pleasant quiet man, and his wife Jeannie were supposed to be leading production lights, but they were disorganised. There were also a few girl Fridays running about aimlessly. The BBC this was not!

The first day was such a disaster that Ernie and I called an emergency meeting to which we invited Dave Armour, Nick Olchowey, Jeannie and Annie. We put our cards on the table, explaining that, although we weren't criticising them personally, it would be impossible to put a successful production together unless some major changes were implemented – including putting a construction plan in place. These charming people weren't idiots, and they saw the sense in what we were saying. During the next week or so *Vince Hill At The Club* began to take serious shape.

Annie dashed off in a taxi to buy some joke books from the local shops, and anything else she could lay her hands on that might help with the script, which Ernie and I now effectively controlled. I worked out the show's format and liaised with Richard Tomkins, the scene man and a remarkable sculptor and artist with whom we socialised a great deal. Then I passed on my song suggestions to poor Ernie, who burned the midnight oil drawing up the scores. One problem he faced was a union rule stating that he could only use musicians from a specific catchment area: this was troublesome in that the standard wasn't what he would have liked. Dave Armour was a good pro and quickly adapted to working alongside Ernie, assisting with his personal script and also the general one. Meanwhile, Nick Olchowey and Jeannie proved to be more than capable once they knew which way they were going and what they were supposed to be doing. Things were definitely looking up, but it remained a daunting task. It's thirteen hours of television we're talking about, and it all had to be completed in six weeks. The chances of us making the deadline were improving by the day, but then fate reared its ugly head – threatening to sabotage not just the production but my entire career, and even my marriage.

I've always been a one woman guy. This is neither a boast nor an idealistic principle; I believe it's rooted in good fortune and the way the cookie crumbled. I met the woman I wanted to spend the rest of my life with when I was barely out of my teens, and we've been happily married for fifty years. Because I've been so fortunate I'm somewhat slow on the uptake when it comes to recognising the come-on signs from a member of the opposite sex. Annie's amazed me in recent years with stories of ladies, well known and otherwise, who she knew were an 'absolute cert' had I been that way inclined. Rather than seeing it as some sort of masculine compliment, I actually find it embarrassing. Annie saw Terri Scott coming . . . but predictably I didn't. The strangest aspect of the whole episode was that I have no recollection of her ever making a pass at me, even in jest, and I was never alone with her at any time. I've often wondered during quiet moments if I should be re-defined as the *un-consummate* professional.

The first rumours I heard about me and Terri having a romance came from one of the studio's backroom staff, who Annie had befriended. She confided that Terri was telling everyone who'd listen that she was having an affair with me, which went back to the days when we worked the clubs together in Coventry. I'm not completely blinkered and I realised that Terri was a very attractive lady as well as a good singer, but I'd never picked up any indication of her admiration for me. I suspect it might have been an attempt on her part to promote her career if the press got hold of the story. Had this happened we'd both have denied it, of course, but the column inches would have done her no harm at all. What she may not have considered was the damage it could have done to me. Such were the values in Canadian society at the time that my TV contract contained a morality clause, which stated that if I or anyone connected to my party in any way sullied the image and good name of the television company, I'd be liable personally for the cost of the entire production. This would have undoubtedly bankrupted me.

In the event, as far as I can recollect, Annie had a quiet (or perhaps not so quiet) word in the appropriate place, and that was the end of the matter . . . if not the end of my brushes with Canadian morality!

The schedule was so hectic that we were all worked to a frazzle. One day Ernie, Annie and I decided to have an afternoon off and go on a shopping expedition. I always looked forward to these occasions because they were fun and a form of escapism, not least because of some of Ernie's outrageous purchases. On this occasion he decided to buy a new suit. We went into an upmarket tailor in the town centre to choose the cloth and get him measured up. Grabbing the material sample book, which measured about six inches square, he chose a cloth in five minutes flat, and held it up triumphantly with a glint of satisfaction in his eyes. 'Perfect!'

Annie and I looked on in disbelief, and asked as diplomatically as we could if he could imagine what it would look like made up. It was attractive as a small piece half the size of a handkerchief, but to describe it as gaudy would be kind – and as a full two- or three-piece suit . . .oh dear! Ernie was undeterred. He went through the measuring process and was told he could pick it up in seven days. We all agreed to have dinner the following week at our favourite restaurant so he could christen the suit, and we went on to enjoy the rest of the day together.

The great day arrived, and we were getting ready for the celebration dinner when there was a tap on our bedroom door. I opened it, to see Ernie standing there in his new suit looking like, well, at best . . . Max Miller. 'I'm not sure about it,' he croaked, the expression on his face making him look even more comical. 'I think I look like Coco the Clown!'

I did my best to suppress my laughter, but all that came out was a snort that sounded like a Hammer House cackle. I quickly collected myself, and told him to wear it no matter what as it might grow on him, but that only made us laugh. From then on we always referred to it as his Max Miller suit.

During the six week filming period I had to fulfil a whole package of promotional engagements to advertise the forthcoming series, in addition to the daily grind. The TV station executives pulled out all the stops, and long before the filming was completed my records were selling in ever-increasing numbers. As a result of all this activity I was getting more and more press, and some of it was encouraging to put it mildly. Jack Miller in the *Spectator* described me as 'a rare star find' and in another piece said, 'Vince Hill is carrying the TV station's major hopes in TV variety.' The result of all this was to be invited to star in the Gage Park Concert, a major open air event; incredibly it nearly landed the three of us in trouble with the Canadian morality laws again. There was a fabulous orchestra at the venue and I loved singing with an army behind me: it really is the ultimate experience for any singer. Ernie's arrangements were superb as ever, and Annie took charge of several bottles of champagne so we could invite all the front and backstage staff to celebrate in British style after the performance.

The whole show was magnificent, complemented by brilliant sunshine and a wonderful family atmosphere. As Annie lined up the glasses and was about to crack open the first of the bottles, a panic-stricken security officer rushed over towards us. 'You can't do that! You can't do that! It's against the law!' We knew there was a strict no alcohol in public law in Canada, but had no idea it included backstage. This was an open-air affair, though, which made all the difference. Happily it all ended in smiles.

Fate had a final twist which could have threatened my Mr Clean image. When filming was completed, and the twenty-six episodes were in the can, we arranged an informal party in the studio. There was hugging and there were lots of tears. Annie had been into town to buy a small present for each of the crew, and in return they presented us with a silver platter which we still use for wine glasses. Just as we were leaving after the party Richard Tomkins, the artist and sculptor, took us to one side and gave us a large parcel neatly tied with shiny golden string. 'I can't afford a lot,' he said, shifting from one foot to another, 'but thank you for everything. I do hope you enjoy it.' It was a moving moment, and we thanked him profusely.

We swung our hire car onto the busy highway and headed towards our house, wondering what such a large parcel could contain. Annie wrestled with the packaging, I kept on switching my eyes from the road to the parcel and Ernie sat forward expectantly in the back seat. Finally she opened the last of the folds, and gasped.

'There's enough here to qualify us as dealers if we get stopped by the police. We'd get about eight years each.' Ernie's voice was serious. 'Got to be at least five pounds of best marijuana.'

There was a silence while Ernie pondered on conducting the Canadian prison orchestra, I wondered how I'd look with arrows on my stage suit, and Annie wished she'd married the boy next door. That it was a serious situation went without saying. Had we been stopped for even the slightest misdemeanour during the twenty minute journey and the police had done a routine search we'd have been in deep trouble. Fortunately the trip was uneventful and we stole into the house like thieves in the night, shutting out the world with the finality of a cell door.

Late that night three dark and furtive figures, looking for all the world like members of Winston Churchill's Special Operations Executive, made their way to a nearby lake, emptied a large bag into it and slunk away, leaving behind the most relaxed and carefree fish on the planet.

Back on the A40 we were fighting our way through the inevitable traffic. I was brought back to the present when the car in front braked fiercely and I instinctively did the same – but it didn't wake Annie. We'd been on the road for almost an hour and it had been stop-start all the way; the slow motion of the car had made her doze off.

When we got home the routine of breaking bread with Doris passed uneventfully, except that on her customary attempt to swim to the other bank she seemed to travel further than she usually did before giving up and drifting downstream. I stepped forward to look at various tiny landmarks which might confirm my suspicions. An overhanging branch from a willow tree had either grown out towards the river considerably, or she was about to make personal history.

'Go on, Doris!' I shouted, in a manner unbecoming of any self-respecting ballad singer. 'You can do it!'

I was just wondering what the duck equivalent to champagne was when her little head dropped, her body sagged and she gave up once more, drifting downstream with the current. She took a last look in my direction, and I offered an exaggerated and encouraging wave. I often wondered what difference it would make to her life if she did manage to reach the other side; it never occurred to me that it might make a difference to mine. I walked back to the house with my empty bowl, and felt an inexplicable relief that she hadn't quite made it.

CHAPTER THIRTEEN

Fly Down To Rio

I found myself more relaxed than after any of my previous hospital trips, mainly because I was beginning to think there was a real chance that my leukaemia could be controlled with medication indefinitely. Previously I'd viewed 'remission' as a suspended death sentence, just a few extra months for some poor soul, or maybe another year at most. Of course I'd have been grateful if I'd been dying in agony and my pain had been reduced to a manageable level with three more years to boot: it would all have been simpler to comprehend if I'd felt ill in the first place. A lack of symptoms made the whole thing menacing and incomprehensible, and my imagination had a field day – usually heading for the worst case scenario. Now I finally understood how lucky I was that my condition had been diagnosed early, and the consistently encouraging assessments from medical professionals added to my confidence.

'There are some wonderful holidays being advertised in Rio de Janeiro.' Annie was reading from a holiday magazine. 'Do you remember how we'd always wanted to visit the place, but when we got back we vowed never to return?'

We travelled to Rio in the early '70s, and initially fell in love with the people and the country. A closer look, though, completely changed our views, at least with regard to the system. The contrast between wealth and poverty was horrendous and the corruption was sinister and frightening. Annie and I had no plans to return, but

Ernie had a slightly different view. He met a handsome, bronzed Latin guy called Armando who helped to bring peace into his life for the first time; but that's another story.

Rio de Janeiro is famous for its festivals, and none more than the Rio Song Festival. In 1969 Manchester-born Malcolm Roberts, who had a UK hit with 'May I Have The Next Dream With You', was invited to represent the UK in the competition, and it brought him massive adoration from the music-loving population. Such was the nation's reaction that he was a monumental act to follow. Imagine my surprise when Franklyn Boyd, on behalf of the songwriter Clive Westlake and his publishing company, requested that I should be the singer for the following year's UK offering, 'Out Of The Darkness, Into The Light'.

The Rio Song Festival began for us with a reception at the Brazilian Embassy in London, where we rubbed shoulders with embassy dignitaries, organisers of the contest and music publishers. There was a great atmosphere and it got us off to a brilliant start. We departed from Heathrow on a twelve-hour flight to Brazil in great spirits, not just looking forward to the competition but also to staying at the Hotel Gloria, which was close to Ipanema.

The song contest was part of a festival lasting three days and was to be held in the splendid Ginasio do Maracanazinho, usually referred to just as Maracanazinho. This is a thoroughly modern indoor arena in the Maracana neighbourhood which is said to hold up to 30,000 people. The Miss Guanabara and Miss Brazil beauty pageants have been staged there, and in the '60s and '70s several international music festivals were staged there.

We were met at the airport by our appointed hostess, Teitei: she was the daughter of a former Brazilian Ambassador to the UK, and truly gorgeous. All artistes taking part in the competition had a hostess who was a close relation to a government official.

The food, the accommodation, everything really, was the epitome of opulence and hedonism. On the second evening we were invited to have dinner with the president. We were driven to the presidential palace in a huge limousine, with four police motor-cycle outriders escorting us. The journey was both exhilarating and terrifying, a high-speed trip that wouldn't have been out of place in a Hollywood movie. We whizzed through the streets of Rio at breakneck speed, jumping every set of traffic lights. If that wasn't enough, the motor-cyclists behaved in the most amazing, bizarre and unexpected fashion. For almost the entire journey they performed like a circus act, executing the most intricate acrobatics and carrying out handstands and various other daring moves at high speed. It took us completely by surprise and when we screamed to a halt in the palace yard we joined in with everyone's laughter, although I suspect that in our case it was hysteria.

We attended several more official functions, lunches and galas, which were enjoyable, but at one of them tragedy struck. Judith Durham of The Seekers was to sing 'Climb Every Mountain', and dozens of photographers gathered on gantries on the first floor, jockeying for positions. Some sort of fracas broke out, and one of them was allegedly thrown over the side; it was rumoured he had been killed. The speed with which the incident was dealt with and then covered up was amazing, just seconds. It was as though nothing had happened and the celebrations continued unabated; but for us it left behind more questions than answers.

The big night arrived, and the atmosphere was so electric it seemed you could have used the energy radiating from the audience to light up a city. As for the sensation that ran from my head to my toes as I walked onto a massive apron extension that stretched above the stage and orchestra, it's impossible to describe. Ernie had added his magic, and my performance went even better than I could have hoped for. Any doubts that I might have had evaporated as the last notes faded, and the audience as one gave me a standing ovation, with a noise that hurt the eardrums.

There were some terrific performances, encompassing professionalism and exoticism, and it was a breathtaking evening's entertainment. The biggest thrill for me came at the end when it was revealed that I'd won the popular audience vote by a country mile. Sadly disappointment followed when the official panel voted differently, amid rumours of vote-rigging and corruption. It may sound strange but I wasn't in the least upset. I was a working pro who had 'torn the roof off' a giant auditorium, and I left the place feeling it was a job well done.

There was still some sightseeing left to do, but with hindsight I think the trip would have been more pleasantly memorable had we flown home immediately after the contest. On the last full day Teitei arranged a tour, which she had cleverly devised herself, that took in the Corcovado. The tourist brochures suggested that 'It is almost impossible to conceive a trip to Rio de Janeiro without visiting the statue of Christ The Redeemer', and I have to agree that its majesty is awe-inspiring. However, Annie, already troubled by the incident the night before, was further affected by Rio's poverty – which we clearly saw for ourselves as we journeyed to the statue. The easiest route is via the Corcovado Railway, the first ever electrified Brazilian railroad. Built in 1884, it is even older than the statue of Christ – and it carried parts of this statue to the top of the hill over a four year period. It seems appropriate that it almost exclusively carries the thousands who visit this incredible monument today.

The trip takes twenty minutes. We had barely started when Annie spotted the first squalid dwellings, which weren't even worthy of being described as a shanty town. They had been built next to the railway and spread out of sight. While some corrugated iron was in evidence, most of them seemed to be built of cardboard. Every society has its share of poverty, and I read recently that even now a quarter of our own nation's children live below the poverty line, but poverty has varying degrees of definition. Few would dare to compare conditions in Western Europe with what we witnessed on our journey to see the statue of Christ the Redeemer. It was almost as though God himself was leading as many consciences as possible to bear witness.

En route we were told dreadful stories of children being murdered to make the limited food stretch further, cardboard shacks that melted when it rained, child beggars who have never slept in a bed, and all of this alongside a splendour that is almost beyond belief.

On the return journey Annie told Teitei she wanted to visit the settlements. Teitei's reaction was one of great trepidation. She explained that encouraging outsiders (especially important guests of the state) to see or make contact with the slum dwellers was seriously frowned upon by the establishment. Annie persisted, and Teitei finally relented, but refused to take us there by day, for fear of being seen and reported.

We approached the cardboard township by moonlight, and we headed deep into it, our passage illuminated by lamps using cheap oil or fat and firelight. The burning oil had a pungency that seemed to taint everything, and the flickering effect was hypnotic.

Teitei pointed out a hut where witchcraft known as Macumba was practised. This was the name used for all Bantu (African) religious practices which were predominant in Rio in the nineteenth century and still exist to this day. Annie and I had been married eleven years at the time and had been told we would never have children, but one of the tribal leaders, in a Macumba trance, told Annie she would have a baby boy within eighteen months. We shuddered when we recollected that night after Athol was born a year and a half later.

A sudden wet and hairy shape forced itself between my arm and torso and, startled, I jumped at least half a yard and swung around to face my tormentor. Teddy, my Old English sheep dog, looked up at me as he often did when indulging my strange human ways, and I sighed with relief.

'Sorry, Teddy,' I said, glad to be free of the Macumba. 'Do you want your dinner?' We had saved Teddy from the Old English Rescue Centre in Lincolnshire. Teddy had obviously come from a family, because if he was roaming around our garden and spotted a mum and dad with children passing by, he took up the rear and followed them home. One day we had a telephone call from Henley-on-Thames, which is three miles away. A kindly gentleman explained that he'd been on a long summer walk with his family, and by the time they'd realised the dog was following them there was nothing they could do other than take him in.

I suppose every dog lover thinks his own canine is the cleverest, but Teddy was certainly no duffer and I never had to teach him anything. I just talked to him in normal tones as I would to a sensible child, and he did exactly as I asked. 'Come here, Teddy.' Never a second bidding. 'Go and find Mum.' Off he'd trot. 'Go and get your dinner.' I'd be with him in the lounge, and he'd go out to the kitchen. 'Is that somebody at the door?' Off he'd go to check. When we were going out he always sat expectantly by the door. If he couldn't be part of it I'd say, 'Sorry, I can't take you on this one, Teddy boy,' and he'd respectfully park himself at the bottom of the stairs in the hallway to lie on guard. At night time for the whole of his life he slept in the doorway of the room we were in. If I'd been doing a show somewhere and dozed off in the chair, then the doorway to that room would be his place. When I woke and went upstairs to the bedroom he followed. These were only little things, but they were comforting and dependable.

If I had to describe Teddy's most outstanding characteristic, I'd say that he was a very proud dog. Towards the end of his life he couldn't keep himself clean and I had to do it for him. He was so humiliated, and I could see it in his eyes. Sometimes he looked at me as I was cleaning him, and it was as if he was asking why I was putting him through it.

It took several weeks of pain and suffering for all of us before we decided with heavy hearts to end dear Teddy's pain. I cried, Annie cried, and I think Sagamore cried too.

CHAPTER FOURTEEN

Break Up And Break Down

Although I'm semi-retired, and have been so for a year or more, I still do cabaret and charity shows when requested. Despite contracting leukaemia I recently returned from Blackpool, where I appeared on the North Pier. Nowadays my pianist is Ken McCarthy, who's been around for some considerable time. He took over from Phil Hinton who in turn replaced Ernie Dunstall, when he left to work for Joe Longthorne. My other mainstays are drummers Paul Shepherd and Kenny Hebden and bass players Steve Smith and Phil Berry. When Ernie left me after two decades it was like going through a divorce. Not only had he been like a brother to me, but he was idolised by Annie too: it was the most awful time. It's hard to explain to those who aren't familiar with the business, but there are unwritten rules which all singers and session musicians accept. One of the principal ones is that if the main man isn't working on a Monday night and someone offers the keyboard player a job, then he simply goes and does it without recrimination. Naturally it's different for a star at the very pinnacle of his or her fame, because then retainers are paid and your relationship's exclusive.

I was very fortunate with my career, because what I did was a world away from the rock/pop music stars, many of whom have a hit record and then disappear. My success, as a result of three or four records in particular, gave me enduring popularity that lasted for almost twenty years. In cabaret I performed a floor show that always had a theme and generally lasted two hours, but could be tailored to suit. Requirements varied dramatically, from the *QE2* for example to major and minor theatres, massive working men's clubs and smaller ones, but all paying well. Long after my records ceased to enter the charts I continued to work live at the highest level, and topped the bill at major venues all over the country. As the years passed, however, they inevitably began to decline in status and regularity.

The decline of the variety and cabaret industry wasn't sudden: it was a slow process that took many years and probably dates back to radio first helping to fill music halls, then aiding and abetting their demise, together with the emergence and inexorable rise of television. In the immediate post-war period, before every home had a television set, cinemas were packed and theatres were full. Local village halls all over the country had something on almost every night, and they were accepted as community social meeting places. As television became more successful and widespread the music hall audiences diminished, and the club scene became a major source of live entertainment. Sadly, this was the beginning of the end for variety, with huge numbers of clubs closing down everywhere and putting an entire industry out of work. All that remained for seasoned variety performers were the bare bones outlets, such as pantomime, cruises, minimal summer seasons (already suffering as a result of the guaranteed sun Mediterranean alternatives) and circuses. The purists among us like to think that variety has not so much died – but is enjoying a nap, perhaps! It's extraordinary that radio, no matter how styles change, somehow always manages to retain its status quo.

Younger and slightly different variety-type singers emerged, and some were hugely talented with a wide appeal. One of these was Joe Longthorne, a great talent who could pack a theatre at will. I had my own Radio 2 show for quite a while, *Vince Hill's Solid Gold Music Show*, and one week Joe was one of my guests. He came up to me afterwards and complimented me on my musicians, asking if I knew that he used some of them from time to time. I did, of course. Shortly afterwards Ernie told me that Joe was offering him and some of the others silly money to join him permanently, and he wanted to take advantage of it. I was terribly upset at losing my right tonsil, and it took a while to completely get over it, but show business is like that and life has to go on.

Just then my attention was caught by a feature in the morning paper about a top sportsman who'd had a mental breakdown of sorts, and was having to give up much of his glittering career as a result. It was just crossing my mind that he should pull himself together and stop acting like a big girl's blouse when I remembered my own experience, and immediately felt guilty.

Annie had an awful time during her pregnancy. We shared the trauma big-time. Hindsight is a wonderful thing, and I could see clearly now that my state was partly caused by my need, no doubt exacerbated by showbiz demands, to drive myself to achieve as much as I could as well as I could. I reflected back on hundred-hour seven-day weeks over many years before the news that Annie was pregnant. I never wanted to dwell on the miscarriages that came before the doctors told her we would never have children. Then there was wonderful news, followed by the real possibility that I would lose one or even both of them, then a tumour, and now . . . would the baby survive? I began to walk around in a daze, barely knowing what day it was, just going through the motions. I assumed that all expectant parents suffered in the same way.

But one day I couldn't cope any more. I was about to begin rehearsals at the Royal Court Theatre in Liverpool, where I was to star as Buttons once again, and had arranged to meet director Ross Taylor during the afternoon in the café at Fortnum and Masons in Piccadilly. In the morning I'd been at the studios recording *The Charlie Chester Show* with the BBC Big Band, and after seeing Ross I had to get back to record *Night Ride*, which was extremely popular at the time. The café was a great place: all the theatrical types seemed to meet there and it was nothing to see 'immortals' drinking and whiling away the hours, talking to each other in luvvie-speak and relaxing, quite oblivious of the world around them. There was no such pleasure for me this day.

I'd felt unwell from the moment I woke up. For some considerable time I'd been enduring panic attacks of varying degrees of severity, and my doctor had prescribed valium. This had certainly helped, but the tablets were becoming less and less effective as time went on. I could see now that my workload over so many years, together with irregular food, had left me with little resilience, and probably insufficient mental strength to deal with a trauma as potentially devastating as the one I might be facing. Losing the baby would be catastrophic for both of us; losing the baby and Annie . . .

Ross was waiting, and asked if I wanted a glass of wine or a coffee. I stuttered and stumbled over the decision, sat down, stood up, and eventually just said yes, wiping the perspiration from my brow, only too conscious that it was returning as fast as I could remove it.

'Now I've got these two lovely talented boys who make a wonderful horse with their skins on, and they'll tow you onto the stage dressed in your Buttons finery in the most spectacular way. Then you say, "Hello boys and girls, and . . ."'

All I could think about was my whole world falling apart. Here was this complete idiot talking about little boys who looked fabulous dressed up as horses and describing me in some imaginary gaudiness . . . and my wife and baby were going to die!

I struggled to my feet, spoke words that neither he nor I could possibly have understood, then staggered down the stairs and out into Piccadilly. I was aware of a mighty pressure trying to burst its way through the top of my head. It made me breathless and the pain was excruciating. I felt myself rolling from side to side as I walked, my entire balance out of sync. Although I was walking forwards I felt my feet were travelling in reverse – and still the force was attempting to explode through my skull. I stumbled into Piccadilly underground station and managed, more from instinct than anything else, to get on the right train and head for home. I shuddered at the recollection.

A couple of weeks later a friend said to Annie that she'd seen me one afternoon on the tube, and I'd been reading the *London Evening News* upside down all the way home.

Eventually, of course, Annie gave birth successfully by caesarean, but by then my problem was too deeply rooted and it somewhat overshadowed poor Annie and her troubles. She had to sack the nurse we'd hired for a variety of reasons, and faced up to the ordeal alone. I'd lost control and fortitude, and was incapable of doing anything. I was carefully choosing shows that were recorded, because neither of us trusted me to work live any more, and when *Top of the Pops* came up for my new chart entry 'Look Around', which any self-respecting artiste would have given their eye teeth for, I picked up the phone to cancel it. Annie had a blue fit, dosed me up with valium and off I went. I'd love to see the recording, if it exists, just to see how well hidden a psychological disorder can be.

My condition became sufficiently serious for me to be referred to a Harley Street specialist, and I went off to meet Dr Wier. Wier was a Scot and sounded just like Dr Finlay; from the moment I met him I expected him to call for Janet at any second – but this was the nearest I got to humour. At one stage he considered a therapy called the sleep treatment, in which the patient is put into a controlled sleep for a week or so, then slowly brought out of it. The idea was to give me a complete break from the worries of the world, and a 'grand rest to boot' as the doctor described it. In any event I didn't need this as I slowly began to improve. Although the whole process took a long time, I made a full recovery.

I looked back at my morning paper, and felt empathy and pity for the sportsman!

CHAPTER FIFTEEN

The Queen Mum, Princess Margaret And Me

After finishing with the sports pages I scanned the rest of the paper, but saw little to attract my interest. There were the usual crimes, drug scandals and falls from grace through drink, and brief mentions of the royals. Seeing the faces of the new generation of Windsors got me wondering how long it would be before they developed into real characters, in the way of their forebears. I took a deep breath and began to recall my royal memories.

I met Her Majesty the Queen Mother, appropriately I felt, in the most elegant of theatrical surroundings, the Theatre Royal, Drury Lane, on a night which is the highlight of the show business calendar and surely the most eminent variety show of all: the Royal Command Performance. For some reason this major honour had always eluded me, and although I would have never complained or aired my views, I was terribly disappointed. Then, completely out of the blue, my agent Colin Berlin from London Management called me in, sat me down and announced that my turn had come. There was to be a special theme on this particular occasion, 'The Magical World of Musicals', and by all accounts I was the perfect choice because of the 'Edelweiss' connection. 'Apart from that, the Queen Mum's doing it this year, and you're her favourite singer.' The voice came from Billy Marsh, who had gate-crashed proceedings to get some papers from Colin's desk, and I smiled along with the fun.

'He's not joking,' Colin echoed after Billy left. 'I don't know where it's come from, and we're probably the last to know, but the source is adamant: the old girl's a Hill fan!'

The big night was an extra special thrill for me because of what I'd been told, and Her Majesty certainly was attentive afterwards in the most regal of ways, but I still wasn't completely convinced, even though the rumour persisted. It was many years later that a member of the royal household confided in me that the rumour was true. There's one thing I can most certainly confirm: I was definitely a fan of hers.

Over the years I've met many of the royals. Princess Anne was delightfully snooty, but genuine and businesslike, and Princess Alexandra actually named three of my albums that she had in her collection. Princess Michael of Kent is known universally as Princess Pushy, although I found this far from true: in reality she's a most beautiful and stunning woman. More recently I met Her Majesty the Queen at a Buckingham Palace garden party. We spoke for several minutes about painting and my friend Rolf Harris. She was kind enough to say she enjoyed my singing, and I joked that Rolf earned more from his talents. We both laughed and enjoyed the moment, and I remember thinking how very lucky we all were not just to be part of a democracy but to have our wonderful royal family. The detractors can say what they wish and move abroad if they don't like it, but metaphorically speaking I will stand resplendent dressed as a cavalier forever, feathers in my hat, waving the royal flag.

Princess Margaret, or PM as she liked to be called, had a soft spot for me. I know this because years after our first meeting a lady in waiting mentioned it innocently in a relaxed moment between sips of expensive wine. Naturally I assumed she was referring to me as an entertainer, but Annie had a different take on it altogether.

The first time I met PM was at a charity show at the Theatre Royal in Windsor on what transpired to be a most peculiar evening. It was during the infamous three-day week, a time of political upheaval, when power cuts were frequent. Max Bygraves was to go on first, do his stint, then introduce me. Max will be remembered as one of the industry's music comedy greats, and his popularity should never be underestimated or forgotten. He was at the top of the profession long enough to entertain several generations. While records like 'You Need Hands', which was a massive hit and 'You're My Everything' were songs that most balladeers would have loved to get their hands on, most of us would have run a mile from 'You're a Pink Tooth Brush, I'm a Blue Toothbrush' and 'The Ballad of Davey Crockett', although perhaps not from the rewards. He was a marvel, who seemed to charm his way into people's hearts at will, and could bring tears of sadness and laughter in the same few minutes.

On this night Max was going to need all his skills, and we were all in for a difficult time. He had just gone on stage to introduce the show and do the warm up when the lights went out! Always the pro, Max seized the moment and harnessed the natural human reaction to sudden total blackness with a quick-fire joke about the electricity bill, immediately lighting a cigarette lighter he'd taken from his pocket. It seemed to light up the whole stage. The barmy modern health and safety brigade would have loved his next move: he encouraged everyone in the audience who had a lighter to bring them to life and join him in singing 'You Need Hands'. The effect was electric. Then he turned a tear into laughter by segueing into 'You're a Pink Tooth Brush'. After a couple of throw-away lines it was my turn.

As soon as the reality of the situation had sunk in, I'd gone into a huddle with Ernie to discuss our predicament. We'd planned twenty minutes with the orchestra, who couldn't see to read their music and had retired to dressing rooms or the pub over the road. I felt that clammy feeling beginning to creep up the back of my neck, when suddenly I thought of 'Soliloquy' from *The Sound of Music*: that would take my designated time as near as damn it, and Ernie, superb pianist as he was, would give of his best under the circumstances. Two minutes into the piece and the lights went on, shattering the atmosphere I was playing to, and I had to work twice as hard to readjust the musical ambience. I was incredibly grateful when it was well received, but it's true to say I came off stage exhausted.

Afterwards Princess Margaret walked slowly along the line, shaking hands and chatting. When she got to me she reached out with the tiniest and most delicate hands I've ever seen, and didn't let go until she finished speaking. 'I really enjoyed your performance, and the lights provided an interesting challenge, did they not? What a long song you had to do.' She released her tender hold and moved on. It was a small, insignificant moment, and went unnoticed by all except Annie.

'My God! She fancies you,' she said immediately afterwards, but I honestly thought she was joking. Unfortunately she wasn't, and it led to a most unpleasant period in Annie's life.

Laurie Holloway and Marion Montgomery were a husband and wife team who provided show business with not just an enduring marriage but one so crammed with musical talent and ability that it was mind-boggling. Laurie, the *crème de la crème* of the upper echelons of musical direction, was sought after by the like of Liza Minnelli, Dame Cleo Laine, Judy Garland, Anthony Newley and Stephane Grappelli, and toured the world as Engelbert Humperdinck's musical director. Marion was a jazz singer who may not have had a hit record as Cleo Laine did with 'You'll Always Answer To Me' in 1961, but was nonetheless influential, and I always think of her as being a singer's singer. Even members of the industry who weren't into jazz couldn't help but be impressed by her incredible professionalism. Marion was a class act. In her early days she worked in a Philadelphia nightclub. When a fight broke out on one occasion it quickly turned into a riot. Looking for a way out, she noticed the safest place seemed to be the stage – so she decided to stand there and sing. Had she not, we might not have experienced this amazing performer.

Laurie and I worked together frequently over the years, and it was as a result of this that Annie met Marion. They became the best of friends. Marion was born in America's Deep South and had the most wonderful southern accent; I for one loved to hear her speak. A close friend of Marion's was Princess Margaret. One of PM's favourite pastimes was a relaxed sing-along party around the piano at Laurie and Marion's house at Bray, Berkshire, usually with Laurie tinkling the keys. One afternoon Marion rang to invite us along, and we happily agreed.

We'd been to their home before. There was always a wonderful buffet and great company, and this transpired to be an informal gathering with few guests, though all were recognisable. Frankie Vaughan was talking with Johnny Dankworth and Cleo Laine, while at the far end of the room PM, flanked by two minders, was in deep conversation with agony aunt Claire Rayner. On reflection the mind boggles, and I smile at the field day the red tops would have had with that one. We were welcomed by Marion and Laurie, and then by a lady in waiting, who escorted us over to PM. Before we joined her I caught her eye, and returned her smile. Her eyes never left mine, which with someone else in different circumstances would have been unremarkable, and as we arrived in her company her beautifully tiny and slender hands reached out and held mine gently. The introduction was friendly but formal, and the lady in waiting introduced Annie too. Margaret's eyes never once left mine, and she completely ignored Annie despite the neatest and tidiest of curtsies. We spoke for a while, and then she seemed to spring into life to ask if I would sing a song that she had seen me perform on a recent television show as it was one of her favourites. Eventually I established that it was Cole Porter's 'You're The Top', a song I'd performed publicly many times, and with Laurie at the piano I sang directly to her, holding her hands as part of the song's presentation.

I thought little of it. Singing love songs to other people's wives and girlfriends was what I did for a living, I saw it as a game and thought they did too. As soon as the moment passed and Margaret wandered off, Annie whispered in my ear, 'If she hadn't been a member of the royal family and I wasn't a lady, I'd have kicked her in the tits!' I turned towards her abruptly, expecting to see anger, but what I saw were tears and hurt. 'She hates me, Vince, and what's more I know why.' It would have been hard not to detect a note of indignation.

I knew this wouldn't be the end of the saga, and I was proved right. Soon further invitations to Marion and Laurie's home followed, and predictably they followed the same pattern. Annie had to put on a brave face, which she did admirably. I played the game, that's what I did best . . . I sang love songs.

Time passed, and Marion rang again. There was to be a select party in aid of charity at the American Ambassador's residence in Regent's Park. Princess Margaret was to be his guest of honour, and I was invited as part of the cabaret. 'Please come, both of you.' Marion knew the score, as she and Annie were friends: it was a difficult position for her. I respectfully attended, with an even more dutiful Annie. This time the guests were different, but PM was as pleased to see me as ever and met me with the greeting, 'Don't forget to sing my song.' Annie went through all the royal protocol and procedures, including a respectful acknowledgement for the invitation. PM blanked her appallingly, and even spoke over her last few words while still looking at me.

We enjoyed a wonderful sit-down dinner. I was placed next to PM and Annie sat next to the Ambassador's wife. Normally we would have taken this in our stride, but this time I felt for Annie. Thankfully the meal passed relatively painlessly, although I was starting to get a bit paranoid. Luckily we met some new people, and were able to chat to old friends too. Then it was show time, and those of us who were there to sing prepared discreetly with Laurie, although nobody seemed to want to go on first. In the end it was Marion who volunteered, and when it came to my turn I tried to get in first with a different song. 'I've got a lovely song for you, Ma'am,' I said to PM, perhaps too keenly. 'It's one of Jerry Herman's, "I Won't Send Roses", and I've prepared it especially for you.'

'I hate it! I hate it!' was her immediate response. I hesitate to say she screamed the words, but she left it in no doubt that Jerry Herman had wasted his time writing the song as far as she was concerned.

'But, Ma'am . . .'

'Sing me "You Are The Top" – I know you know all the verses!'

I nodded to Laurie, and he struck up. PM moved in closer, I held her delicate hands, she looked at me, and I looked at her as I sang the words . . .

You're the top!
You're the Coliseum.
You're the top!
You're the Louvre Museum.
You're a melody from a symphony by Strauss,
You're an Ascot bonnet,
A Shakespeare's sonnet,
You're Mickey Mouse.
You're the Nile,
You're the Tower of Pisa,
You're the smile on the Mona Lisa.
I'm a worthless check, a total wreck, a flop,
But if, baby, I'm the bottom you're the top!

Margaret drew me slightly closer – and Annie's eyes bored a hole in the back of my head, but her smile slipped not once. Annie was winning on points, but as it turned out she should have quit while she was ahead. She found herself chatting for a while with Margaret's lady in waiting, and asked her where the ladies' powder room was. The kindly lady offered to show Annie the way, and they set off together up a flight of marble stairs, enjoying their conversation. They went through a door into a section with upright chairs in front of ornate and well-lit mirrors, and Annie went on to the cubicles, leaving her companion seated in front of a glass. She had barely entered a cubicle when she heard the most frightful commotion from the powder room she had just left. Finishing hurriedly, she quickly returned towards the sound of raised voices. There, standing arms akimbo, eyes flashing and spluttering with rage, was Princess Margaret. She stopped her rant momentarily, turned and screamed at Annie at the top of her voice, 'What are you doing here?'

Annie was completely taken aback, but recovered quickly. 'Well . . . I've just used a cubicle,' she said as serenely she could.

'But what are you doing *here*?'

'Finishing up,' offered Annie innocently. 'Your lady in waiting was kind enough to show me to the ladies' powder room.'

'But what are you doing *here*?' The voice was even louder, Annie took a deep breath, turned on a tap, then washed her hands and dried them.

'But what are you doing *here*?'

Annie was now sure she detected a note of madness. She walked slowly towards Margaret and spoke quietly and directly. 'I'm washing my hands. Don't you wash yours when you've had a pee?'

She left the room, head in the air, heading for the marble staircase, knowing she had won the moment. Maintaining her pace and dignity on the long descent, she couldn't resist looking back over her shoulder to see if there was any sign of her tormentor. PM was just about to take the first stair down, and to Annie's delight she looked flustered. Now Annie felt even better. She turned back . . . and her heel caught in a crevice. Up in the air she went in a tangle of arms and legs, and landed in a heap in front of everyone. She told me afterwards that there was one saving grace. She'd bought a new designer dress for the occasion, and had been advised not to wear any knickers so as to avoid 'visible panty line'. As she fell her legs went up in the air, and she was extremely relieved she hadn't taken the dresser's advice.

Some time passed without any invitations, and I suspected I was out of fashion or favour. Then unexpectedly a request arrived for me to take part in a charity function at the Grosvenor House Hotel in Park Lane: Princess Margaret was to be the guest of honour, dancing was to be to Joe Loss and his orchestra, and I was to be the cabaret. Had my agent Dave Forrester not already committed me by saying I was free on the night in question, I might have sidestepped it, given the problems of the past – but the fact that the invitation included Annie suggested peace in our time!

The papers were often unfair to some of the royals, and at one time PM's relationship with Roddy Llewellyn inspired many column inches. Annie was pleased for her, or for herself, and was looking forward to the possibility of an improved reception. As it turned out, the problem didn't arise. Annie decided to put discretion ahead of valour, and although she enjoyed the show and mixed freely, she did so at a respectable distance from PM.

It was a well-attended function. Joe Loss stamped his class, and I received an excellent reception – not least from Princess Margaret and her table, which I spotted out of the corner of my eye. I completed a fifty-minute spot on the biggest of stages, which was capable of making the bravest showbiz heart feel the fear of isolation, and I have to admit I was pleased when I had completed the long walk from centre stage to the wings.

It's impossible to describe walking off any stage to the sound of your own feet, and many seasoned professionals who've worked the northern clubs tell terrifying stories of having done so regularly. The danger in my case was whether the audience applause would last for the length of time it took to walk from the microphone to the wings: it's an entertainer's thing, but you can't begin to imagine the feeling if it doesn't. I'd just come off to a huge ovation, which lasted until I was well out of sight, and was both delighted and thankful. Imagine my horror when I caught sight of PM's new beau bounding across the wide expanse towards me like a startled deer. I knew what he wanted.

'Come back! Come back! PM wants to thank you personally at once!'

I can see him now, adrenalin pumping, eager to please, absolutely no understanding of a performer's logic or protocol, and me looking back over the runway-sized stage at her table in the distance. Traipsing all the way over there wasn't the worst aspect: it was the return journey. I knew all eyes would be on me and her, and then on me alone as I clip-clopped across the stage in an embarrassing silence.

Arguing was futile. Off I went, following Roddy like the proverbial lamb to slaughter, trying to appear as if this was the norm. I attempted to nod in friendly fashion to those who were sitting in silence, craning their necks in an effort to figure out why I was hurrying after my excitable guide. Mercifully I finally arrived at PM's table.

'That was marvellous. We all enjoyed it very much. Will you join us for a drink?' PM's eyes shone, and I realised for the first time how pretty she was.

I accepted the offer, someone moved and I sat next to her with a glass of wine. We talked small talk and laughed at things I can't recall; then others joined in too. It was always made perfectly clear when the time had come for you to make an exit, and this occasion was no different: I got to my feet, made my excuses and looked to see if there was any way of escape without having to navigate the huge expanse of stage. There wasn't, and any chance that there might have been disappeared when Roddy Llewellyn stood up and moved his chair, leaving the huge stage as my only retreat. For a fleeting moment I wondered if perhaps he knew more about showbiz culture than I'd given him credit for; he certainly hadn't missed PM's gaze.

I did a great many more shows for Princess Margaret, and we laughed together more times than I can remember. She held my hand frequently, and when we spoke I searched her eyes for secrets I never found. Annie's views were clear. Feminine intuition is widely recognised, and a powerful counsel, but for me – always in search of the quiet life – I'll always put the Queen Mum, Princess Margaret and me in my private enigma file.

CHAPTER SIXTEEN

Maggie May . . . Or May Not . . . And Shows Galore

I started to clear the decks in the kitchen ready to try out another of Marguerite Patten's brilliant recipes, and spotted the late Teddy's lead hanging in its usual place by the side of a cupboard. We both wanted another dog eventually, but it seemed disrespectful to do so too soon and unthinkable to use his lead. I stuffed it deep into the bin. As I did so I caught sight of a picture of Matt Munro in a recently discarded newspaper, and it reminded me of Ian Bevan.

I'd always felt indebted to Ian Bevan from Harold Fielding's office, ever since he saved me from the contractual clutches of Bertie Green which had cost Matt so dear, but when he called me up and asked me to support the Conservative Party, well, I wasn't so sure. I'd always considered politics a private thing, probably because of how I was brought up, and I was taken aback. I didn't respond immediately: my mind raced as I considered the audience reaction, and whether I had a responsibility to my fans. The people who bought my records and paid to see my shows might disapprove if their views were passionate and at odds with mine, so should I remain impartial?

The fact was that I had working man roots, and there was a great deal about Labour politics that was synonymous with my early years, but I was beginning to think that times were changing and Labour ideas were getting left behind. Then suddenly there was Maggie Thatcher!

Ian explained that he'd been approached to handle a Conservative Party public relations exercise at which their leader would be introduced at the forthcoming Conservative Trade Union (CTU) rally, to be held at the Wembley Conference Centre. The idea was for me to sing her onto the rostrum with a special song. 'It'll cause a sensation.'

'But will Maggie like it?'

'Maggie may, or may not, but we're doing it anyway!'

Ian went on to add that the media coverage promised to be excellent, and that at some stage I'd be joined by the singer Lulu. The idea was to obtain permission from writer Jerry Herman to pen a new lyric to his standard 'Hello Dolly', and the general consensus was that I should be the singer. I'd re-record the song, and then on the big day I'd sing the new version as Margaret Thatcher walked out to meet her adoring supporters.

I gave the whole thing a great deal of thought, and finally made a decision. The more I thought, the more I realised that although my roots were at odds with it, I was a Tory through and through, and didn't see why those who enjoyed my music should hold it against me. 'I'll do it,' I said to a delighted Ian Bevan, and less than a week later I was in the studio recording the track. The opening lyrics are worth a mention:

> *Hello, Maggie,*
> *Well hello, Maggie,*
> *Now you're really on the road to Number Ten.*
> *You're going strong, Maggie,*
> *Won't be long, Maggie,*
> *Till you turn that key,*
> *Then, Mrs T., you'll . . . see Big Ben.*

The CTU Rally was an amazing affair, with an atmosphere only equalled by a concert given by the most revered of stars. Margaret Thatcher was a phenomenon, and a legend in her time. If ever this mood was captured by the media it was now. That night and the following day every TV, radio and news programme covered the event, and every national newspaper had Wembley on its front page, with pictures of Maggie plastered everywhere. And of course I was in all of them. If we'd run off together there wouldn't have been more coverage. It was an absolute sensation and it ran and ran.

There are references to my recording of 'Hello Maggie' being played in all sorts of obscure places, and at least one that suggests it was played on one of the occasions when she met her friend and confidant Ronald Reagan in America. It took a long time for it not to be the opening line at every meeting I had, with just about everybody, and it's a talking point to this day. And it wasn't the end of my involvement with Tory Party politics.

Some years later Ian was back, and this time it was to celebrate another major Conservative occasion. The theme for this latest epic had been inspired by a song called 'Hundreds of Girls' from *Mack and Mabel*, another Jerry Herman musical which had run on Broadway. There were many different versions of the lyrics, but one of the verses I recall went like this:

> *Four girls on a slide*
> *Five on a swing*
> *We're gonna make*
> *The cash register ring,*
> *It's Maggie, yes, Maggie for me.*

Annie and I went on to enjoy more than one dinner with Margaret Thatcher at the House of Commons, often with our great friend MP Sir Philip Holland. One thing is for sure: I'll never be able to say that my foray into politics was bad for business, and I never cease to be amazed by the power of publicity.

Having dispensed with the morning paper I turned to the junk mail, and it was on its way to the bin when I spotted an advertising banner: 'They Sold a Million'. I scanned the contents, only to find it was the usual record compilations, and quickly dispatched it. But it got me thinking of Nigel Lythgoe.

I was contracted to front BBC2's *They Sold A Million*, which was a kind of songwriters' show in which they told the stories behind the hits. It was a completely novel approach which proved popular. Nigel Lythgoe, who went on to become Mr Nasty on ITV's *Pop Idol*, was the choreographer behind the all-singing all-dancing Young Generation, which we affectionately dubbed YG. He did a splendid job. YG were much loved and went on to do much more afterwards.

The show contained a great deal of biographical stuff, and although its popularity was widespread it also developed a cult audience who were fascinated by the trivial facts, and we received letters to that effect. I was still recovering from my breakdown, and unluckily I had a great deal of script to learn word perfect every week. I'd have welcomed an autocue, but the producer insisted it was out of the question – which seemed wholly unreasonable, all things considered. The show had two excellent scriptwriters in Roy Tuvey and Maurice Seller, and they had a brief to put an emphasis on using as many descriptive sentences as they possibly could. For example, I'd have to say, 'When World War One wore its weary way to a close . . .' or 'The Goddess of the silver screen in this gargantuan box office bonanza . . .'. Having to memorise masses of this, with no hope of an idiot board, was difficult and an unnecessary strain.

Thirteen shows were scheduled, and we were well into them when producer Stewart Morris sent word down that he wanted a bigger presentation that I thought bordered on overkill. He was insistent that the words written by Roy and Maurice had to be delivered with an emphasis that a circus ringmaster might use, or maybe a DJ frothing at the mouth on a Saturday night. I didn't see that it was appropriate and said so. Then came the dreaded call: Bill Cotton, the big white chief, wanted to see me.

I'd no sooner walked through the door when he said, 'The singing's good, but the talking's crap! I'm going to extend the run from thirteen to fifteen shows and get it onto BBC1, so I'm going to bring in Terry Wogan to help with the workload and give you space.'

Even after all these years I still feel the sting. 'But that'll just make me look stupid. How do you plan to salvage me?'

'You'll open the show, as ever, then introduce your pal Terry, and it'll go like a charm.'

Then came the twist. It transpired Mr Wogan would use the autocue for the whole of his presentation. I was miffed, because if I'd been given that assistance I'd have been able to address Stewart's need for more emphasis. It just wasn't fair, but then life isn't, is it?

There was, however, a small comfort during the first session. Stewart looked down from his vantage point, took one look at Wogan and shouted to his studio manager, 'Get that bloke into something that makes him look a bit less like a bank manager, will you?'

It would be silly to deny that there was friction between Terry Wogan and me, and in fairness I did little to ease the tension because I felt I'd had a bad deal and probably resented his presence, but I didn't do myself any favours in the long run. Terry was a big radio and TV personality with lots of air time, and he never played a Vince Hill record ever again. It probably cost me a few bob in the long term.

Shortly afterwards the show changed its image and was renamed *The Musical Time Machine*, this time produced by Terry Hughes, who later went to America and produced *The Golden Girls*. The idea was for me to operate a futuristic music time machine referred to as Hai Fai. I'd talk about a song with a camera in front of me, and as I tapped the details into Hai Fai the lens would close in on the screen. Then the technology would mix it through to the YG on the studio set, where they'd perform it. Somewhat ahead of its time, it was a great effect and was a magical approach.

Marguerite Patten's recipes had always been my favourite distraction when I needed to escape from something unpleasant, and today I was going back to Hammersmith Hospital. I'd risen early and was asking myself which I'd spent more time doing recently, swotting up on my recipes or looking back over my career. As I leafed through one of Marguerite's specials I was actually thinking about *Gas Street*, which almost seemed like a betrayal of the great lady – and at the very least slightly unsavoury.

Gazing through one of Marguerite's pages, I remembered the phone call from my agent asking if I would like my own chat show. I gave it very serious consideration for a hundredth of a second, and replied in the affirmative. It was to be called *Gas Street*, produced and directed by Bob Cousins and Sid Kilbey, and based in Birmingham. It was to be a midday affair, and initially there were to be two pilot shows, which was fairly normal for new formats.

Annie was ready, and we set out on a journey that was getting to be too much a part of the normal itinerary for my liking. I wondered for the umpteenth time how long it would take the medical experts to determine my treatment, and the prognosis.

The waiting room at Hammersmith Hospital was getting too familiar. I had my favourite chair against my favourite wall, and I always did the same things when I got there. Annie sat down and I went to get us both a coffee, having got the right change when we bought the newspaper at the hospital shop. I sat down, looking suspiciously at my magazine: it had a tear in the same place as the one I had put down a fortnight before. I read a line, or less, then closed my eyes and returned to *Gas Street*.

Gas Street is a very famous part of Birmingham and now a tourist attraction, but it hasn't always been that way. During the nineteenth century, when Midlands industry was at its height and the waterways were their main source of supply, as many as a hundred barges passed through the city of Birmingham with their cargoes every day. There was what amounted to an industrial war, with bitter rivalry between companies fighting for trade, and the canals weren't always linked by the shortest route. In Gas Street Basin there exists to this day a bar which separated two competing firms from encroaching upon the other's network. *Gas Street* seemed a perfect title for a place where I could meet my guests in the middle of a working day.

The chat show was to be presented twice weekly: I would do the Tuesday and Suzi Quatro the Friday. The format was fairly straightforward and the show, while intended to appeal as a lunch break for the busy working housewife, also catered for shift workers and anyone else who had access to a television set in the middle of the day. Guests were often famous actresses, like Beryl Reid, with whom I sang 'I Remember It Well' from *Gigi*, Dora Bryan and Millicent Martin, but there was often a serious side. For example, I entertained the likes of journalist John Pilger. John was one of only two Australians to win Britain's Journalist of the Year Award, his documentaries had won Academy Awards on both sides of the Atlantic and he was revered by his peers. We didn't neglect light entertainment either. One day we welcomed club comic and impressionist Johnny Moore and a lady called Barbara Waller, who was a tortoise enthusiast, which as you can imagine slowed things down a bit. Immediately following Barbara was Josette Simon, who had just appeared in *Cry Freedom* alongside Denzel Washington and Kevin Kline. This was Richard Attenborough's film about the black South African apartheid leader Steve Biko, and was his second biopic, following the Oscar-winning success of *Gandhi*. Johnny Moore performed two or three routines, and I finished the show by joining him in a comedy song. It was a huge range of entertainment. *Gas Street* ran for six months, and was an exciting and enjoyable experience.

The sound of my name being called transported me back to the present, and I opened my eyes and stood up, 'You're seeing Professor Apperley today. Please come this way.'

Jane was her usual bright, breezy and professional self, and although she wanted to take some more blood she explained it was simply routine. There was some good news. My body seemed to be responding well to the medication I was taking, and subject to the results of the current tests she expected to be able to give me some kind of prognosis on my next visit. The appointment was over very quickly, and for the first time there was definite hope on the horizon. I unquestionably felt more optimistic than on previous occasions and, light-hearted, I suggested that we should drive into Reading for a pub lunch. It was very pleasant. As we were leaving a large man walked by smoking a cigar, and in a split second I was transported to the *QE2* with the unforgettable George Burns.

Entertainment for the passenger liner *QE2*, the flagship of the Cunard Line for almost forty years, was booked for much of that time by agent Gary Brown. One day he called and asked if I'd like to work it for a week, picking it up at Hong Kong and cruising down to Singapore. My immediate reaction was, 'God, Gary! It's a twenty-hour flight to pick it up and a hell of a long way to go for a week's work. And it means I'll have to cancel two shows I've got in the book . . .'

'You'll be working with George Burns,' Gary interrupted.

'Where did you say I pick it up?'

The fabulous George Burns was a legend in so many lifetimes that it's confusing. Born in 1896, George died in 1996 – and only narrowly missed keeping his promise to play the Palladium when he was a hundred. He began his showbiz career in vaudeville and covered radio, television, film and more cabaret than anyone will ever know about. He became more famous at the age of seventy-nine than ever before thanks to the Warner Brothers movie *Oh God!* In this he played the part of the Almighty as a good-natured old man, opposite the country music singer turned actor John Denver.

Meeting George Burns was everything I could have hoped for, and much more. I'll never forget his opening words. He leaned forward, as if to indicate that he was about to share something confidential with me, and said in his deep unique tone, 'I'm pleased to meet you, Vince. They tell me you're a very genuine young man.' Then he leaned even closer. 'If you can fake sincerity you've got it made.'

When we stopped at Singapore I decided to go and visit Johnny Hawksworth, an old friend from the Ted Heath Band days. He was a pianist and bass player and was playing at a jazz club there called the Pigalle. An hour or so before we set off George asked where we were going, and I mentioned the Pigalle Jazz Club.

'I'd like to come,' he said in his quiet drawl.

I hadn't the vaguest idea what the place was like: it could have been a dump for all I knew. I hadn't seen Johnny for years and had no idea what to expect. The thought of taking the great George Burns to anything less than a class joint filled me with dread. 'Let me suss it out first,' I begged. 'If it's all right we'll come back and fetch you, OK?' He nodded.

I needn't have worried, as it turned out. The club was excellent, the music terrific and we were in good company, enjoying lots to drink and having a great laugh, when one of the lads in our group announced he was going to find the gents. When he came back he looked subdued and his face looked strained.

'What's the matter?' I enquired.

He held his glass up and looked at it against the light, then put it to his nose and sniffed at it. 'You'll never believe it, but I think I've just seen George Burns in the bog,' he said uncertainly.

Just then the entire room went silent and we turned around to see why. There, standing in the doorway silhouetted by an overhanging lantern, giant cigar in mouth, was George. There followed the most amazing scene I have witnessed in fifty years of entertaining around the world. The entire room stood as one, and began a standing ovation that lasted several minutes. It began with clapping hands, and by the time it was in full swing everyone in the room was shouting and cheering. George slowly walked over to us, sat down and turned to acknowledge the applause, then in his usual style he moved closer and spoke directly into my ear. 'Years ago I used to get an ovation when the act went well. Now I get one for being alive.'

A year or so later George came to London to do some filming and stayed at the Ritz in London with his girlfriend Kathy and her daughter. He telephoned me to arrange a meeting and we agreed to have dinner together, but unfortunately he was called back unexpectedly by the production company to re-shoot a scene, and as a result couldn't make it. 'Would you take Kathy and her daughter?' he asked. 'I'll send a limo.' Naturally we were disappointed he wasn't joining us, but agreed.

The limo arrived, and Annie and I decided on Langan's Brasserie in Stratton Street. We arrived in magnificent style, thanks to George, and we were looking through the menu when

Kathy's teenage daughter spotted Status Quo sitting at a nearby table. Shortly afterwards I popped to the gents and the lads were in there having a good-natured laugh, which developed into one at my expense – especially when one of them asked me for my autograph for his grandmother.

'You should go on tour like us,' one of them said. 'We make more now than we ever did when we were selling all those records.' I began to explain that it was quite different in our side of the business, then realised they were winding me up: all good fun but no contest.

We had a splendid meal, then paged the limo, having agreed to give Kathy and her daughter a tour of some of London's lights by night. Quo were outside discussing where they had left their cars, and the leg-pulling started again. It continued while our uniformed chauffeur opened the doors for each of us in turn. I was enjoying the fun, even if it was one-sided, when suddenly one of them pointed to the rear of the sparkling limo.

'I think the laughs on us,' I heard him say. My eyes followed his pointing finger. 'We usually hire one of those only when we want one,' he concluded.

We looked at the limo's number plate together. It read VH 1.

I've pondered the mystery of the VH 1 registration plate for many years, and have never been sure if what so impressed Status Quo was a remarkable coincidence or an incredible, albeit inexplicable, piece of generosity by George Burns, as improbable as it might be. Then, three decades later, I met a man who had worked in the premium car hire business at around the time the incident occurred, and he told me a remarkable story. Over a three-year period in the late '70s and early '80s a fast-thinking mover in London's West End offered limos and expensive chauffeur-driven cars for short hire at extraordinarily inflated prices. These prices included personalised number plates. The cost was extortionate, but the service was extremely popular for those with big wallets who were out to impress their guests by having their initials on the expensive hire car. The scheme was simple, but illegal. Appropriate bogus plates were fitted, no questions were asked, and the driver took the risk of being apprehended in return for a handsome reward.

Given that the real plates were underneath and it could be explained away as a joke if it was discovered, it was a lucrative scam – and by all accounts no-one was ever caught.

I'll never know, of course, but I can say without doubt that if there was one man I knew on this planet at the time with such inimitable style it was George Burns.

I looked back casually at the man disappearing into the distance whose huge cigar had transported me back to my time with George, and wondered if he would live to be a hundred.

There are a number of special characters who, like George, stand out in my memory, and one that comes to mind is actor-comedian Dickie Henderson, who enjoyed great success until his death at the premature age of sixty-two in 1985. I worked with Dickie many times. We became firm friends and there are a hundred stories to tell. He could be dynamic on stage and was amazingly versatile, but off stage he had a dry sense of humour that was somewhat similar to George's. He often growled out hilarious one-liners or punch lines, and the expression on his face was almost as funny as the gag. One Saturday night we were both booked for an important show at the London Palladium and Dickie, who loved a drink, always had a bottle of something in his dressing room. As was customary, I popped in to see him before the show and he offered me a glass. I generally had a drink of something sparkly, but because of the importance of this particular night I decided to abstain. 'No thanks, Dickie. It's an important night. I don't think I should.'

He turned his head slowly towards me, tilted it on its side, and in a slow, deep drawl spoke words that I'd remember affectionately forever. 'You mean . . . you're going on . . . alone?'

Dickie was born into a show business family and had a father with the same name. Dickie Senior performed at a Royal Command Performance and Dickie Junior did too, exactly thirty years later. No mean family feat.

The Dickie Henderson Show ran from 1960 to 1968, and was a family format that was likened to *The Dick Van Dyke Show*. Opposite

Dickie, playing his wife, was June Laverick; his fifteen-year-old screen son was John Parsons and later Danny Grove. The series was hugely popular.

I have lots of London Palladium memories. I particularly remember having a three week run there with Shirley MacLaine, although it has to be said that both comic Lennie Bennett and I soon got to wondering why we'd been booked in the first place. Shirley was the ultimate song and dance queen, and I'm not sure if to describe her as the consummate professional does her complete justice. Her commitment was absolute, and no-one in her dance company was ever left in any doubt if a routine was anything less than perfect. At the slightest error I've seen her rant like someone possessed, walk off stage, gather her wits and concentration, and return to begin a whole section over again. It would be wrong for me not to mention what a fantastic person she was, and what a privilege it was to share the stage with her each evening – even if only briefly!

The show began with Lennie coming on and doing the warm-up spot. This usually developed into twenty minutes or thereabouts, and he then introduced me, to complete the first half with my forty minute spot. Gradually Shirley's production routine grew to such an extent that Lennie's offering came down to ten minutes and mine to fifteen – but even this doesn't tell the whole story.

Some months before, Shirley had completed a UK tour so successfully that she couldn't wait to repeat it, and Dick Katz, part of my management team (and incidentally a former pianist with Ray Ellington), was approached to this end. Dick envisaged a variety format, and put me and Lennie into it, not knowing that Shirley viewed the show quite differently. The Shirley MacLaine Show, as far as she was concerned, was all about Shirley MacLaine, and she had neither need nor desire for makeweights. Her production would fill the entire two hours, and given the magnificence of her performance she was probably right. I even remember Annie wanting me to pull out of it altogether, as there was too little time allotted for me to produce anything of any consequence. All's well that ends well, and we played to packed houses every night, which placated everybody and went a long way to prove that Shirley was nobody's fool.

*   *   *

Back to Sagamore and the present. Later that afternoon I did my customary once a week inspection of the orchard, and thought back over my American tours, principally at the Florida performing arts centres – which is what the Americans call theatres. I had a great time in Clearwater, Tampa and Lakeside, and it was a great feeling to appear the week following such names as Jack Jones and Neil Sedaka. An even greater thrill was singing with the seventy piece Florida Symphony Orchestra: I can't begin to describe the sensation of fronting such an amazing ensemble.

I'd just got to Florida in my mind's eye when I spotted Doris Duck in the orchard with a couple of her cronies. I'd picked up a spade with the intention of shovelling away the rotting, although not entirely unpleasant-smelling apples, when I caught the concentration of her stare. I decided to leave them. After all, I wouldn't want anyone destroying the contents of my wine cellar!

CHAPTER SEVENTEEN

Death Threats In Kuala Lumpur

Kuala Lumpur, the capital of Malaysia, has a population of 1.3 million and lies in a central position on the Malay Peninsula. The city developed quickly after 1873 with a major expansion into rubber and tin trading, both of which remain vital to its economy today – although food processing, cement-making and the manufacture of electrical goods are also important. And they just loved my TV show *They Sold A Million*.

The show was very popular in Malaysia, and as a result it was almost inevitable that the call would come to pay the country a visit. I'd been booked to appear on Australian television and then appear in New Zealand, so my agent Dick Katz suggested that I took in Malaysia on the way. The deal was an excellent one. Dick would be paid half the fee in advance in England by Universal Promotions, who were based in Kuala Lumpur, and the remaining half would be paid to me just before I went on stage, while all expenses were to be paid as well. Together with Ernie Dunstall, we arrived in Kuala Lumpur after the long flight, and were held back from disembarking. Because of the presence of hundreds of frantically screaming girls, we thought that some rock group or other was expected – so we decided it was safer to remain in our seats until the aircraft was almost empty, then edge our way slowly forward. As we did so the noise grew louder and louder and louder, and then I detected some of the words being screamed in English: 'Mr Millions, Mr Millions, we love you, we love you, Mr Millions, Mr Millions, we love you, we love you!' There were literally hundreds and hundreds of girls, and they were all there for me. I didn't know quite how to react. It's obviously a great honour to be welcomed in such a way, but this was completely alien to me after spending much of my career in the rather more sophisticated cabaret side of the business. Normally the nearest I got to kids screaming at me was when they got tired after, and sometimes during, pantomimes.

Eventually we were greeted by an EMI welcoming committee, and I signed autographs until my hand nearly dropped off. Getting past all the girls was a huge ordeal, but I eventually succeeded, and we arrived at the Hilton – to discover that we had the whole of the top floor penthouse suite. I started to wonder how The Beatles and the like managed to deal with this kind of reception all the time: the strain of that kind of adulation must be immense.

Our luggage still hadn't caught up with us and, anxious to shower and change, we rang reception to enquire where it was. An hour later we were told it had arrived safely in Australia. I was flabbergasted! The good news was that I had one of my stage suits together with my orchestrations in a large hand luggage case, but we had to send out for a great many bits and pieces. It was going to be a long four days.

The hotel was fabulous, the people absolutely charming and the city captivating, but it was hard without our luggage – particularly for Annie. Soon the day of the show arrived and we set off to the stadium venue, which was packed to the seams and heaving with about ten thousand people. We were accompanied by two Indian officials from Universal Promotions, and about half an hour before I was due on stage I asked for the balance of the fee – as arranged. One of them said they hadn't brought the money with them, as it wouldn't have been safe; so Annie had to accompany them back to the hotel for payment to be made in full. When this was complete, she would telephone me at the venue. I didn't like it, but it was a Catch 22. If I didn't go on when they had a sensible reason for not having the cash at the venue, then arguably I was in breach. On the other hand, if Annie went back and didn't get the money, I'd worked for nothing. In the event Annie made the decision to go back with them.

While I waited with increasing nervousness, poor Annie went through a living nightmare. They travelled the short distance back to the hotel and went up to the penthouse suite, where she was alarmed to see the tallest Chinaman she'd ever seen sitting on her bed – with a suspicious looking bulge under his jacket. One of the Indians locked the door behind them and leaned against it, and while he picked at his nails with a grotesque looking blade the other told her in a sinister tone that she was a hostage, and she would stay there until they were ready.

Annie played hell and made threats of her own, but there was little doubt in her mind that they meant business, and she'd be lucky to get out in one piece. She made the point that if I didn't hear from her I'd refuse to go on stage, and they'd lose the upper hand. This seemed to cause them a great deal of irritation, and the huge Chinaman kept banging a hand on his knee in the most hideously sinister fashion. Annie was petrified, but also frantic with worry at what might be happening to me. For my part, the Universal Promotion representatives who'd remained at the stadium assured me that the only reason I'd not received Annie's call was because the phone lines were down, and I must go on to fulfil my obligation. What neither Annie nor I knew was how the system worked: money was collected from ticket sales at designated points and the Universal Promotion crooks (as Annie now knew them to be) were buying time while they picked up the cash just ahead of the bona fide collectors. It transpired that all ticket sales were through major retail outlets in shopping malls, and at a pre-arranged time the money was collected by authorised personnel and allocated appropriately. In effect a bogus collection operation was taking place, and the crooks holding Annie were part of the getaway plan. Annoyingly we were unaware that the previous month the Bee Gees had been turned over in similar fashion. No-one, it seemed, had thought it worth warning Dick Katz, and as a result death stared Annie in the face.

Back in our hotel penthouse, where invasion of privacy and

breaking and entering seemed to have paled into insignificance against kidnapping and hostage-taking, Annie's indignation and threats didn't exactly make her the perfect prisoner. Occasionally her captors argued heatedly in their own language, and at one stage the Chinaman reached inside his jacket, leaving no doubt that he was threatening the Indians with a firearm. Annie couldn't speak or understand Indian dialect, but she kept hearing the same words repeated, '*Amar mone hoche ore mere felte hobe*'.

Finally, almost three hours after Annie had left the stadium with her two Indian companions, a telephone rang in the penthouse suite. After a brief conversation Annie was tied up roughly by the wrists and the three villains made their escape. This was far from the end of the affair. None of the expenses had been paid, and we had to pay an astronomical amount for the penthouse and all the other extras that should have been part of the deal. The police did little, and we weren't unhappy to leave Malaysia.

For Annie a reminder lingered for many years afterwards. At the time of the kidnap she was wearing a new lightweight maroon silk coat, and her ordeal had been so terrifying that all her clothes were drenched in perspiration. When she was packing she noticed that a complete section of the coat had been bleached almost white: she had often heard the expression 'smelling fear' and described this as actually seeing it. She kept the coat for many years as a reminder of her brush with death.

As if we hadn't had enough problems during our short stay, I managed to pick up some sort of stomach bug which had kept me on the run for several hours before we departed and during the flight to Australia. Dehydration set in, and although I was drinking plenty of water it wasn't improving. I was glad of some medication that a doctor prescribed at the hotel. I decided to double up on the dose and it began to have some effect, although I still felt rotten. As we settled down in the aircraft Annie beckoned a beautiful Asian flight attendant over. 'If I wrote down some sort of Asian language phonetically,' Annie said, 'do you think you might be able to give me a rough translation?'

'I'll do my very best,' came the reply.

I watched curiously over Annie's shoulder as she wrote. The attendant took the piece of paper, studied it for a moment, then responded with a sharp intake of breath. 'I read of your ordeal, Mrs Hill, and I'm terribly sorry for what happened to you, as indeed everyone must be. You had a narrow escape. These words are Bengali, and roughly translated they say "We may have to kill her".'

CHAPTER EIGHTEEN

The Irish Connection

I shivered at the thought of what might have happened, but simultaneously chuckled at the thought of a magazine article that described my clean cut, laid back, unexciting, nothing much ever happens image. I'd certainly had my share of adventures, but there had been some laid-back stuff too.

Arriving in Australia after the Malaysian ordeal coincided with my birthday, and Annie wanted to give me a special treat. We were booked into the Sebal Town House Hotel, which at that time was frequented by entertainment industry personalities, the rich and otherwise famous. We were instantly pleased to meet Cleo Laine and Johnny Dankworth. I was excited at the prospect of appearing at the Sydney Opera House, where they were already performing.

The Opera House has to be one of the most iconic pieces of architecture ever constructed, and is described as Australia's culture portal. Opened in 1973, work had first begun in 1959: few would argue that the fourteen year wait wasn't worth it. On the site of the Fort Macquarie Tram Depot, it's on Bennelong Point which stretches out into the harbour – and and the view of it from the air is both dramatic and unforgettable. It's instantly recognisable: there's nothing like it anywhere else.

My first appearance was on the popular chat show hosted by Mike Walsh, which gave me an opportunity to get my feet under the Australians' table, so to speak. From there I moved on to Surfers

Paradise, where I was booked for two weeks at the Twin Towns Club. Next stop was Brisbane, where I had the privilege of meeting Frank Bellet who, it transpired, was something of an admirer of my work. A few weeks earlier he'd produced a radio documentary of my life and times, and the interview and some of my records complemented it – and seemed to work very well.

Then came my birthday treat. I've always been a passionate follower of David Attenborough's wildlife films, and especially the series that was filmed on Heron Island. Imagine my delight when my present was a trip to the very place where the filming had taken place. It proved to be a long journey, and took three separate aircraft as well as a private helicopter, but it was the highlight of the trip – making up for some of the Malaysian trauma for me, and going some way to helping Annie too.

Finally there was the splendour of the Sydney Opera House, the magnificence of the 2CH Radio Orchestra and the thrill of being the focal point on the stage of one of the wonders of the world.

Another place I love, but in quite a different way, is Ireland. I love the country and the people, and especially their sense of humour: the way they laugh at themselves endears them to me most of all. Some years ago I was working in Dublin at a place called the Clontarf Castle Hotel, but all you needed to say to the taxi driver was Clontarf and off he'd go, telling you his life story on the way. On this trip the cabbie began immediately with the blarney. 'Ah, Vince, 'tis lovely to have you back again in Oirland. Jeez, oi do love the sound of yer voice!' He then told me a hilarious tale of how he was mistaken for a famous singer when he was out one night, but his accuser couldn't remember the celebrity's name. To be helpful, the cabby decided to make one up. 'Oh, oi'm Vic Evans,' he said, puffing out his chest.

'That's it!' exclaimed the excited man. 'I knew yer were famous, can oi please have yer autograph?' As far as the cabbie was aware there was no such singer as Vic Evans, but he dutifully signed anyway and thought that was the end of the matter.

Two nights later he went into a Dublin pub and, one chance in a million, there propping up the bar was his biggest fan, telling the story of how he had met the famous Vic Evans. Before the cabbie could make his escape the fan spotted him and bounded over, dragging him back into his company and introducing him all round to an eager bunch. 'Please would yer be givin' us a song, Vic?'

'Oi really can't, me dear friend,' said the cabby, forced to keep up the pretence. 'Oi've been touring all over America with dat very famous singer Paddy Riley, and oi'm truly knackered. Oi can't raise a note.'

Now there really was a singer called Paddy Riley, and unfortunately for the cabbie he was in the very same pub. 'What a stroke of luck,' everyone chorused. 'Yer man's over there. Now yer can both sing us a song.'

My driver was now in a proper pickle, and went over to Paddy, bought him the best drink in the house and guiltily explained his dilemma, adding that he was tone deaf. Paddy, being a gentleman, having a sense of humour and loving the craic, kindly got him out of trouble by agreeing they were both very tired after an exhausting, and couldn't possibly sing – but would they accept a drink from two famous singers. My cabbie was off the hook. I swear it could only happen in Ireland.

The truth is you really do have to take in the whole Irish experience to fully appreciate their native fun and the spin they put on it. I'm convinced that more often than not the Irish appearing to be stupid is actually them poking fun at the rest of the human race. You have to observe it first hand to acknowledge its incomparable nature.

For example, once I arrived at a venue and was pointed in the direction of the dressing room, only to find that the door had a notice on it saying 'PULL', but no handle. At another there was a piano with no pedals and, would you believe, I was once on a bill with a supporting pianist – but there was no piano for him or for Ernie to play. 'It has to be a grand,' I insisted.

'Don't you be worryin'. It'll be the grandest piana yer ever did see.' And several willing Irishmen pushed one on its slender runners half a mile from the nearest nunnery! Another night I was signing autographs when a lovely rounded Irish lady with a glint in her eye told me how much she'd enjoyed the show. 'Did you? I'm so pleased.'

'Yes, beJasus, yer can make dat feckin' voice speak!' I think I know what she meant.

On another occasion at Clontarf I encountered a difficult audience, and it took all my skill and experience to get them into the swing of things. I was delighted to finish with them all on their feet. Afterwards I was doing the customary signing session when a lady came up and said, 'Well, yer were good alroight, but whoi didn't yer sing the songs you sang at the end at the beginning? Then yer'd 'ave bin bloody fantastic.'

Another time, going by taxi to the Clontarf, a different driver told me he was a karaoke singer and had lost his voice one night. His doctor told him to take milk of magnesia. 'For your throat?' I asked incredulously.

'To be shure,' came the reply. 'Troi it, Vince. Cost me fifty quid to foind that out and it's yers fer nothin'.'

Some weeks later I was a bit hoarse, and being a bit of a worrier I thought why not: it might be a miracle cure. It did nothing for my voice that I can be certain of, but it's a good job it was only a short walk from the stage to the lavatory! I should have known better. Only in Ireland!

CHAPTER NINETEEN

Sierra Leone And
This Is Your Life

After retreating from the duck's wine pile I decided to do an exterior inspection of Sagamore. Early twentieth-century property is much sought after, but you have to keep your eye on it – and I'm proud of the fact that I've always done so.

I scanned the roof, shielding my eyes from the brightness of the sky, and was pleased to see everything was as it should be. Then I turned towards the river, distracted by a nearly new medium-sized cruiser heading upstream. I could see a young couple on board, obviously in love and enjoying each other's company. She was heavily pregnant. It reminded me of how blessed we were to have eventually had Athol, but I also reflected on the miscarriages that poor Annie had suffered along the way.

After one particular ghastly experience her doctor insisted she got away from it all, and packed us off on holiday to Sierra Leone. We arranged with Annie's wonderful mum Evelyn, known affectionately as Evie, and my father-in-law George to move into our house and look after Athol for a couple of weeks, so Annie really could get away from any distractions. The doctor had given explicit instructions that we were to be incommunicado other than in extreme emergency, so you imagine Annie's panic when two days into the trip I took a call in our room from London. I barely managed to say 'Vince Hill' before getting disconnected. 'Athol, Mum or Dad's had an accident – I just know it,' she wailed.

Unfortunately the telephone system in that part of the world was fairly primitive back then, so it wasn't just a matter of dialling back. Then Lady Luck took a turn. Conservative MP Sir Philip Holland was staying at the same hotel, and when he heard about Annie's dilemma he offered assistance. 'Come with me to the British Embassy,' he said, 'and I'll see if I can get you a line via the diplomatic link.' To say we were delighted was an understatement, and off Annie went with Sir Philip to pull a few strings.

I didn't know, and Annie had forgotten, that the *This Is Your Life* team had decided to have me as one of their subjects, and were well into the planning. The production team was in place and Annie was well into the research, but the whole thing had to be a complete secret, of course. Apparently a problem with the broadcasting date had come up and they wanted to put it back a couple of weeks – so they wanted to discuss this with Annie. When Annie got through to her mum she was full of apologies, but under the circumstances she'd had no choice but to give the production head our telephone number. When I answered he'd hung up, to avoid giving the game away. So now all Annie had to do was explain to me what had happened when she got back to the hotel – and with Philip Holland's help she managed to do this superbly. One good thing came out of the whole episode: Philip and his wife Jo became firm friends.

The holiday was over all too soon, but naturally we were pleased to get home to Athol – and of course Annie had clandestine *This Is Your Life* work to do. I was blissfully unaware of everything, although I had the occasional niggling thought at the back of my mind. Annie was my business manager, and while she conducted this with a minimum of interference from me, I pretty much knew what was going on. Then suddenly she needed to go places alone or with our secretary. If this wasn't worrying enough, when telephone calls came in she'd walk out of the room, blaming the sound from the television – but this had never created a problem before. Was my Annie having an affair?

On one occasion, while I was doing a week at Caesar's Palace in Luton, I finished early and arrived home ahead of schedule. As I walked into the hall I heard a great deal of shuffling from the front room, and as I entered Annie and a strange man were hurriedly getting up off the floor to sit on the settee. I noticed at once that his flies were undone. I forget quite how she introduced him, but the fact that he was outrageously camp distracted me from my shotgun. With the benefit of hindsight there were other obvious signs that nothing sinister was going on, but I never cottoned on and the whole thing remained a secret to the end. As part of Annie's role she had to go through reams of pictures, cuttings and brochures for the producer, whose attention to detail was acute. All this had to be achieved without me having the slightest indication of anything untoward, and I realise now that the strain on her must have been enormous.

Three dates were set initially, and they were all deferred for one reason or another. Finally the *This Is Your Life* production team together with Annie put a booking in my diary for a charity event for Help the Aged at the Daffodil Club in Bethnal Green, as part of a purported documentary by ITV. In reality this was where I was to be surprised by Eamonn Andrews and the Big Red Book.

It was much later that I heard of the great excitement that went on the night before, around which the most preposterous yet extraordinarily clever subterfuge was arranged. The *This Is Your Life* team had a bogus invitation put together inviting Annie to the Metropolitan Police Flying Squad Ladies Night, in order that she could attend the final planning meeting at Thames Television's studios. I recall her being very excited when she received the invitation, and thinking that it was an unlikely event for her to be so thrilled about. When she arrived it was with a mixture of relief and pleasure to find that all the guests had arrived safely, some from other countries, so that the director could go through the script, plan the running order and answer an enormous number of questions.

One hilarious moment came when Billy Carroll, who'd been my pianist at the Prospect at Margate, revealed he was going to tell how we shared a bed for a week during the talent competition there. I'd won the first prize, which was a week's engagement at the Prospect, which included accommodation. I'd thought this would be at the pub too, but it transpired that Billy would be putting me up at his place. Now Billy was as camp as a row of tents and lived in a one-bedroom flat. Aged fifteen I'd never heard of homosexuality, and when I was tipped off that he was gay I replied, 'Yes, he's a very happy chap.'

It's probably not widely known that what the guests say when they're introduced is usually scripted by professional writers, but Billy had prepared his own piece. Eamonn Andrews had the greatest difficulty explaining to him that he couldn't be openly gay and then announce in front of millions that he'd shared a double bed with me for a week without it leaving innuendo in its wake. After a very funny half hour Eamonn eventually made his point, and a somewhat bewildered Billy agreed to keep the story to himself.

Finally all the rehearsals were completed, and the production team was happy. Now all Annie had to do was tremble over the night itself.

The big day arrived . . . for them at least. I was in the vegetable garden, covered in mud and planting my potatoes. Naturally I was wearing my oldest trousers and boots, and so engrossed in my activity was I that it didn't seem odd that Annie was interested in the state of my fingernails. I remember commenting that I thought it unlikely the Help the Aged fraternity at the Daffodil Club in Bethnal Green would mind me singing to them with the odd broken nail, but promising to scrub and file them. Even so, I did wonder momentarily about the number of trips she made to the vegetable garden that afternoon.

Ultimately Annie convinced me that as the evening's event was being recorded I should make an extra effort and put on good clothes, rather than arriving in casual dress. This made sense, so I got ready a little earlier than I might have done usually.

Bethnal Green and the Daffodil Club were as far east of the centre of London as we were west, so we allowed a couple of hours to make the journey. Annie was on edge and I thought perhaps she was unwell. When I suggested she should stay at home I received short shrift, and we headed east in silence.

*　　*　　*

I like the East End. I have to admit that in a way it scares me, but it's an admiring, respectful type of fear that's hard to describe. Show business has attracted villains since time immemorial, and I've received my share of attention. I remember when one of the most notorious gang leaders in the North East decided to befriend us, making it clear that all we had to do was ask and we could have anything we wanted. He'd turn up and insist on taking Annie shopping, which she hated, and we started to go out when he was most likely to turn up. Occasionally, though, he caught us out – and it soon became obvious he was sussing out our times in the same way we had his. Often Annie had no excuse, and he would take her around various shops and persist until she agreed to accept some expensive gift or another. What really disturbed her were some of the expressions she spotted from management when he wasn't looking: loathing mixed with fear. The item(s) were always gift wrapped, and they left without money changing hands. She was quite sure she was the receiver of stolen goods, and couldn't do a thing about it without incurring the wrath of a very dangerous man.

One evening we had dinner with him at a smart restaurant. It was enjoyable, despite me getting the impression that a number of distinctly shady-looking characters at another table were looking threateningly in our direction. When our host paid a visit to the loo I primed Annie to feign a bad headache so we could make a hasty retreat. It worked, and he asked a waiter to ring for a taxi. The following morning we heard he'd been badly beaten up by five assailants, who followed him out of the restaurant, then ran him over several times before driving off at high speed. It transpired he'd been very lucky: a month earlier another rival had been beaten to death.

The East End was just as violent, but my experiences suggested it was a little more subtle than the north. The gang leaders left me in no doubt about who they were, however, and frequently reminded other pro entertainers who relied for their living on these criminals to point them out to me. Often it was a direct introduction and the words, 'If you want to work anywhere in particular, Vince, just let us know.' I never did.

It's very hard to feel sorry for serious villains who've committed dastardly crimes when the law eventually catches up with them, but I have to make one exception. John Redgrave, a director friend who was the most amazing lighting expert I've ever encountered, was once a prison visitor. One day we met for lunch, and he told me he'd seen Reggie Kray during a visit to a top security jail. 'Did you know he's a big fan of yours, and listens to *Friday Night Is Music Night* on Radio 2 every week?' he said, smiling. At first I thought he was joking, but soon realised he wasn't. 'Do you think you could spare him a tape, perhaps with "Look Around" and "Edelweiss" on it? Reggie really would be grateful, and he says I might live a bit longer if he gets it.' We both laughed, and I agreed.

A month or so later I received a HM Prisons-headed note written in a scrawl that was difficult to read, but I eventually deciphered it: 'Dear Vince, thanks for your kindness, it will help with the time. Reggie.'

'Turn left for Bethnal Green.' Annie's voice snapped me out of my gangland dreamland and I whipped the wheel around accordingly.

It was obvious it was going to be a serious documentary, because there were enough production vehicles parked at the side and around the back of the club to make a small movie. As soon as I entered the concert room the director introduced himself, and explained he wanted me to be singing one of my songs with Ernie doing the backing, and that they'd pan in and out with a camera over the introduction dialogue. I only got to the end of the first verse before he shouted 'Cut', got into a huddle with some of his staff, looked around furtively and asked me to start again, saying they had gremlins in the equipment. After about five takes I was about to get a bit stroppy when I was aware that a sudden silence had come over the small audience of a hundred or so, and people were looking round in different directions. I commented to Ernie that it was a strange set-up, and he nodded – although he didn't seem fazed in the least.

Now we've all probably experienced the sensation of someone standing in the shadows, imaginary or otherwise, and suddenly I became aware of a presence behind me. I spun round and there, complete with his red book . . . was Eamonn Andrews. I managed one word only. 'Christ!'

'Vince Hill, you thought you were here at the Daffodil Club in Bethnal Green tonight to sing a few songs for a TV documentary, but in fact, Vince Hill . . . This Is Your Life.'

It's hard to describe the emotions when the whole of your professional career is played out before you, not just as a tribute but in your honour. I've always been a perfectionist, and as a result I've never been completely satisfied that I couldn't have done better; the effect of this is a tendency to feel unworthy. I found the experience terrifying, humbling and ultimately completely overwhelming, and I concede that this recognition from my peers was the highlight of my life.

After Eamonn's surprise appearance I was chaperoned by researcher, later producer, Maurice Leanard and taken by car to a venue called The White House, near the television studios at Euston Road. Meanwhile Annie and Ernie travelled straight to the studios. I was treated to champagne while the final touches were made, and then went with Maurice to the studios.

Annie was the first to appear, followed by the Royal Corp of Signals Band who played an introduction, then old workmates from my coal-mining days and from a bakery I'd worked at. Ken Dodd came out of the shadows, closely followed by the magic of David Nixon (the most famous magician in Britain in his day), then my mum, dad and brother and sisters. My brother Jack was introduced in a particularly sensational fashion. Jack, no mean entertainer himself, worked as a dustman by day, and they ran a film of him on his rounds, interrupting him to say a few words to me on film. 'Do you remember singing this with me, our kid?' he said, and broke into song:

There was once a farmer who took a young Miss
In back of a barn where he gave her a . . . lecture
On horses and chickens and eggs.
And told her that she had beautiful . . . manners

That suited a girl of her charms.
A girl that he wanted to take in his washing and ironing
And if she did they would get married
And raise lots of . . . Sweet Violets . . .

I joined in, and so did some of the audience. It ended in mirth, and, surprise, surprise . . . Jack too came in from the shadows.

Julie Rogers was followed by The Raindrops, and Len Beadle – who'd been married to Jackie Lee, of course. He gave Jackie a kiss and remarked that he had 'once known this young lady'. Incredibly she had flown in from Canada. Next my old mates Johnny Worth and Teddy Foster appeared, and, to bring it to a close, my best friend from army days, Brian Mather, at whose wedding I'd been best man and who played trumpet with the Royal Signals Band.

Then we adjourned to a celebration party. It was superb, and crowned an unforgettable adventure.

CHAPTER TWENTY

Death, Life, And The Verdict Was Theirs

I hadn't received a letter for today's hospital appointment: I'd been given a date at the end of my last visit and it was etched in my brain. This was when Jane Apperley would give me her prognosis. I knew Annie had been worried for a considerable time, as you can't live with someone for fifty years and not be able to tap into their thoughts sometimes. People die from leukaemia every day and I had it, so her fears were hardly unexpected. I'd managed to shut it out for most of the time, but when it was hospital visit week my illness came to the forefront, like it or not.

During our journeys to Hammersmith Hospital Annie either made nervous conversation or sat in silence. Today she was quiet, and for once I liked it that way. Today I felt pessimistic for some reason, and I cursed myself for my negativity. It was so bloody stupid. I knew there were thousands worse off than me, but I was the only one I had to deal with. I scratched my head and struggled to think of something that was overcome when all seemed to be lost, and I thought of Ivor Novello.

Born David Ivor Davies in 1893, Ivor Novello was a Welsh singer, composer and actor who became one of our most popular entertainers in the early part of the twentieth century. Both Annie and I loved his music and were captivated by his persona – more specifically the intrigue that surrounded him. Novello first came to prominence when he penned 'Keep The Home Fires Burning' in honour of those fighting in the First World War. In 1917 his show *Theodore & Co.* was a smash, and he went on to have many more show successes. He also wrote songs, and 'We'll Gather Lilacs' and 'Someday My Heart Will Awake' became classics.

It was Annie who thought of the idea of writing a stage play about the life of Ivor Novello. She devised the concept and commissioned Vince Foxhall to write the script. Her energy was boundless. She formed a business association with Patrick Ide, head of the Ivor Novello Trust (INT) and also of the Theatrical Investment Trust, and they set out to attract investment for the project. Various companies showed interest, with McAlpine's leading the way, and Patrick guaranteed finance from the INT. Patrick was also in partnership with Peter Saunders, who was married to Katie Boyle and produced *The Mousetrap*, which has got every chance of running forever.

Annie's and Patrick's production, entitled *My Dearest Ivor*, opened for six weeks at the beautiful Mill Theatre in Sonning and was a huge success, with more than one review mentioning West End potential. It came to the attention of Paul Gane, of the Fortune Theatre, London, who was running *The Woman In Black* – which he didn't expect to last. He decided to look at *My Dearest Ivor* with a view to it being the replacement.

Annie and Patrick took the production to the Theatre Royal, Margate, for three weeks to take off the rough edges, and then to Brighton before a final airing in front of Paul Gane. Then fate took a hand. *The Woman In Black* took off, packing out the Fortune Theatre, and then when Annie and Patrick were leaving a restaurant one evening Patrick fell over and badly gashed his head. Immediately his moods began to change. He and Annie were the best of friends, and the change in him hit her hard. From being in constant telephone touch, eating out regularly and constantly exchanging fun and ideas, contact ceased altogether. Annie was at her wit's end, and we went to his flat on several occasions, leaving notes and answerphone messages by the dozen. In Patrick's absence the cast still had to be paid, and he held all the money in a Bank of Scotland account. There was no alternative: we had to produce the cash.

A month later, still with no sign of Patrick, we went to the police and begged them to investigate his disappearance. They burst into his flat to find that the place had been burgled and Patrick was lying on the floor. He had been dead for some time. An open verdict was returned, but we haven't the slightest doubt our friend was murdered. There were many contributing factors supporting this theory: his mother's ring was missing, as were his father's watch and many works of art which he treasured. In addition, a great deal of the production company's money was missing. One sad fact confirmed Annie's belief that Patrick's head injury had been really serious. The flat contained dozens of unused household appliances he'd bought since the accident: all unnecessary and all unopened.

The cost of that fall was enormous for poor Patrick, and cost me and Annie a great pal as well as £200,000 which we'd loaned to the production while we waited for Patrick to surface. We couldn't afford to lose that sort of money, but we did, and we survived.

This positive thought gave me a little heart as I made my way to hospital. I never burn up the miles, but today I had plenty of time and was in no hurry to hear what Jane had to say. For the first time I took in the scenery, glancing at houses as we passed. Some were boarded up, and I wondered if they'd been repossessed or compulsorily purchased for road widening. I imagined children's laughter and Christmases past, comparing this with today's dark and dank interiors. I read the billboards, seeing beautiful women who'll never die advertising exotic perfumes that will never fade, and magnificent sleek motor cars that use no fuel and need no road fund licence. Idiots overtook, deliberately pulling in tight to show their disapproval at my keeping to the speed limit, while lorries hugged my back bumper.

'Everyone's dying, yet everybody's in such a damn hurry to do it,' I said out loud, 'It's just that some of us are going quicker than others.' I added.

'Don't even think it,' Annie growled. She meant it. I didn't . . .
I was just being silly again.

We drove through East Acton, and Annie said it brought tears
to her eyes to see how the streets she had played in as a child had
degenerated. I wondered if it was her life that had improved while
Acton had stayed the same. I wondered if she'd skilfully deflected
the emotions provoked by my chronic myeloid leukaemia onto the
streets of London.

The waiting room was quiet when we got there. People looked
up curiously as we entered and I smiled at no-one in particular, chose
seats in the usual place and went to get the coffee. We hadn't bought
our usual newspaper, as we didn't want to read about people dying.
I wondered if the relative silence was because everyone was there
for their prognosis, then I snorted at the absurdity of this notion. I
checked in at the reception, and almost at once my name was called
– and the nurse told me I was seeing Dr Marin.

'Meester Heel, how are you? I hope you've been having your
glass of wine? How is ze seeing? I hear one of your songs on za
gold radio za other day.'

He really was the loveliest man, and I had no problem with it
being him and not Jane Apperley.

'So,' he began, looking at a computer screen that told him
everything and me nothing. 'As you can see, there is za maintenance
of the stability of your leukaemia thanks to za medication. I have to
say that I don't theenk it'll be this that'll keell you.'

He looked at me expectantly, and I looked at him even more
expectantly. Then I leaned forward and whispered, 'What is it . . .
that'll kill me, doctor?'

He looked surprised momentarily, then said in a voice filled
with mystery, 'The computer does not tell za future, Meester Heel.
It's a very good seestem but it's not supernatural. I can say almost
definitely that it's unlikely to be za wine that keells you either.'

I felt light-headed and could hear Annie sobbing quietly. It was
as if she was in the distance and I was observing the proceedings as
a fly on the wall. 'Do you mean I'm going to beat this thing, doctor?'
I spoke the words but they didn't seem to be instigated by me.

'It'll be necessary for you to come every four weeks for za tests, but as long as you take za tablets, you'll probably die of za old age, and no time soon.'

The next ten minutes passed in a haze of grateful thanks, with the usual pleasantries and appointment-making. I felt Annie gripping my arm as though she was never going to let e go, and it hurt like hell. 'Vince, please let's go now,' she begged as I dallied unnecessarily, probably as a result of shock as much as anything else. 'You've no idea how I've prayed for this moment,' she faltered, silent tears streaming down her face.

The car seemed to drive itself away from the hospital, and turned automatically into Starvin' Marvin's, a railway carriage-shaped American fast food restaurant on the A40. We were both chattering at once. Annie mentioned going away on holiday and other things we had to do, and I realised that we'd left so much on hold. The meal was great, and when we resumed our journey the scenery no longer seemed drab and cold. The people I noticed were smiling and happy, and I swear the sun came out as we passed the Ruislip turn-off. We decided to have friends over for dinner, and spent time talking about nothing, constantly interrupting each other and chuckling like a couple of daft kids.

Slowly we relaxed, and a calm and pleasant silence said things that words could not. The Jaguar purred like a contented cat, and when we entered our driveway Sagamore smiled.

EPILOGUE

Frequently, when I confided my innermost secrets to Doris, I imagined how it would be if I were to return from hospital one day with the news that I wasn't going to make it. On the other hand, I also fantasised about the words I'd use to tell her the glad tidings that I was going to survive.

I'd found contemplating death a very private affair. I felt it wasn't the right or honourable thing to do to lumber poor Annie with my worst fears, although I told her my superficial worries. She seemed strong, and told me to be brave. Naturally I said I would be, but was then even more frightened of the unknown. To Doris I could say anything: tell her about Bob Monkhouse dying and the flowers I'd bought Annie. She'd just cock her head, look at me quizzically, then swim round in a circle and stare back waiting for more drivel . . . or food. She definitely had feelings, of that I was quite sure. One day Teddy had come bounding up unexpectedly, and she didn't come back for two days. Even then she'd stared at me suspiciously for the first ten minutes.

So here I was on this wonderful day, the very first day of the rest of my life, carefully preparing Doris's grub having made certain that I had at least half an hour to spare to speak to her, and feeling like ten million dollars. I wanted to stand on a rostrum like they do at the Baftas and Oscars, and thank my mum and dad for having me, the doctors and nurses who do what doctors and nurses do, the woman who ran the hospital shop, the receptionist whose mum was a fan, the girl who swept the floors and the bricklayers who built the hospital. I wanted to breathe in the air that had been touched by the summer sunshine, caress every leaf on every tree and kiss every blade of grass, and I never doubted for one second that Doris would be there waiting for me. I was so thrilled as I approached to see that she was there.

I sat down on the bank, and she came straight up to me without hesitation. I whispered to her with tears in my eyes, 'I'm not going to die, Doris Duck.' My hand trembled as I passed her some of the bread I'd bought on the way home from the hospital. She took it gently and waddled to a safe distance. 'Thank you for listening to me so often and for so long, funny little duck,' I mumbled gratefully. 'I'll never be able to thank you enough for your kindness.'

She turned back to face me, and I thought I'd spare her having to come up close by tossing the bread to her. She ignored it, and came back and took the piece I was holding in my hand instead. For all the world she looked as if she was about to say something.

'I've climbed a big hill in the last few weeks, Doris, and you've been there for me when I needed to say silly stuff out loud. I'm so grateful . . .'

There was nothing more to say, and in any case Doris was on her way down to the water's edge. I watched her paddle out slowly into midstream, then further. Without the slightest effort she reached the other side and climbed effortlessly out of the water. I stood speechless as she disappeared from sight, spilling the rest of the bread onto the bank.

I still feed the ducks and they still get drunk in the orchard. I still strain my eyes up and downstream with hope in my heart . . . but I never saw Doris Duck again.

ACKNOWLEDGEMENTS

I don't wish to dwell on hospital visits, doctors' surgeries, blood tests and all that; anyway you have just read about it. So I would just like to say thank you to the people who, over the past seven years or more, have been so much a part of my life.

Chris Eden at the Hampshire Clinic, my GP Julia Milligan. Fenella Brito, Professor Jane Apperley and all at the Catherine Lewis Centre at Hammersmith Hospital. Without your intelligence, compassion and dedication I would not be here ... gratitude is not nearly enough.

The cover picture is by my long-time friend and some-time tennis partner, Bill Mundy, who apart from being a wonderful painter is, like me, a lousy tennis player. Mind you I always win!

Thanks to Nick Charles OBE for his patience, expertise and talent.

Must mention Doris the scruffy duck! Although she is probably now in that great river in the sky, wherever you are Doris, you were a great comfort to me as I fed you your daily bread and talked such drivel to you.

Some names have been changed to protect identities and probably some names have been missed out but whoever you are, wherever you are, thank you.

Finally there is my ever loving other half, Annie, who has had to put up with me all these years and has a memory like an elephant when kicking over the traces. She is my rock, my love and my irreplaceable companion. I love you Annie.

Vince Hill

Lightning Source UK Ltd.
Milton Keynes UK
06 April 2011

170448UK00001B/64/P